Alcohol and behavior
AN ACTIVATED EDUCATION APPROACH

Alcohol and behavior

AN ACTIVATED EDUCATION APPROACH

DARWIN DENNISON, Ed.D.

Associate Professor,
Department of Health Education Professions,
State University of New York at Buffalo,
Buffalo, New York

THOMAS PREVET, Ed.D.

Associate Professor, Department of Health Education,
State University College,
Fredonia, New York

MICHAEL AFFLECK, Ed.D.

Lecturer,
San Francisco State University,
San Francisco, California

Illustrated

The C. V. Mosby Company

ST. LOUIS • TORONTO • LONDON   1980

Copyright © 1980 by The C. V. Mosby Company

All rights reserved. No part of this book may be reproduced in any manner without written permission of the publisher.

Printed in the United States of America

The C. V. Mosby Company
11830 Westline Industrial Drive, St. Louis, Missouri 63141

Library of Congress Cataloging in Publication Data

Dennison, Darwin, 1937-
  Alcohol and behavior.

  Bibliography: p.
  Includes index.
  1. Liquor problem. 2. Alcoholism. I. Prevet, Thomas, 1943- joint author. II. Affleck, Michael, 1950- joint author. III. Title.
HV5035.D45   613.8'1   79-25741
ISBN 0-8016-1252-7

C/M/M 9 8 7 6 5 4 3 2 1   01/D/033

FOREWORD

The alteration of drinking practices—that is what this text is all about.

In 1967 the Cooperative Commission on the Study of Alcoholism released its monumental report, *Alcohol Problems: A Report to the Nation*. In that treatise, a long-term approach to the prevention of problem drinking was offered. The proposed program that sought to modify the ways in which Americans use and sometimes abuse alcoholic beverages was labeled a unique, novel, and even revolutionary means to combat and reduce alcoholism. In this scholarly book Professors Dennison, Prevet, and Affleck have succeeded in presenting an educational format to accomplish the noble and necessary goal of the Cooperative Commission's report—the primary prevention of problem drinking.

By applying the principles of "activated health education" to education about alcohol problems, the authors provide a viable alternative to the more traditional forms of alcohol education. Activated alcohol education focuses on the consumer-student, involves the learner in both formal and informal experiential learning opportunities, identifies and clarifies personal attitudes and values as related to drinking practices, and offers objective information so as to create cognitive dissonance and individual sensitivity to alcohol-related problems.

For many years, alcohol educators have admitted that providing information alone does not necessarily improve drinking practices. *Alcohol and Behavior: An Activated Education Approach* is a sound alternative to the more passive programs that rarely achieve any significant change in drinking practices. However, activated alcohol education will challenge some who have become mired in the information-based aspects of instruction. Yet, because of the active participation of the consumer-student through field and laboratory experiences and because responsible decisions about one's personal drinking behavior are facilitated by this approach, the likelihood of more responsible drinking patterns is increased. The extra effort on the part of the alcohol educator, that is, linking educator-provider and consumer-student activities and providing specific knowledge preceded by experience and followed by application, is certainly justified in terms of the final outcome—positive alcohol health behavior.

Unlike some methods texts and curriculum guides that overwhelm the reader with subject matter content, this book emphasizes curriculum implementation. Examples of field activities and laboratory experiences are offered, along with various learning games, organized discussions, and suggestions for role playing. A detailed Alcohol Behavior Inventory also assists individual drinkers in assessing their own alcohol usage.

Thoroughly documented, scientifically researched, and educationally sound, *Alcohol and Behavior: An Activated Education Approach* is destined to become a significant and vital component of educational programs to reduce problem drinking and promote responsible use of alcohol in a drinking society.

Charles R. Carroll, Ph.D.
*Professor, Department of Physiology
and Health Science,
Ball State University,
Muncie, Indiana*

PREFACE

The majority of Americans use alcohol in one form or another. Most of these persons use alcohol without experiencing problems. However, some users, for a variety of reasons, abuse alcohol. Some Americans engage in dangerous and disruptive behaviors during and after drinking, while others drink reasonably and responsibly.

Alcohol and Behavior: An Activated Education Approach presents the basic scientific and behavioral facts regarding problem drinking and the essential components of activated alcohol education to achieve responsible drinking.

The objectives of this book are (1) to describe and exemplify the components of an alcohol education program based on the principles of activated health education; (2) to provide objective, unbiased information related to alcohol usage and how alcohol abuse may be related to dangerous and disruptive behavior; (3) to provide general information regarding the properties of alcohol and detail selected research on the effects of alcohol upon physical and social functioning; and (4) to provide general information regarding affective activity and specific examples of group activities that lead to responsible drinking behavior.

Alcohol education was developed as a primary prevention program for university students. However, other audiences may include individuals involved in secondary or tertiary programs including health consumers and providers. The program has been successfully implemented in alcohol education programs for nurses, police, and driver education.

This book is based on our practical experiences and research efforts in designing and implementing activated alcohol education programs. The chapters are sequenced to follow the program details in Chapter 1. Health education professionals not familiar with activated health education should read this chapter first. Students and health consumers interested in the scientific and behavioral aspects and not in the intervention procedure might start with Chapter 2. Chapters 2 and 3 define the scope of alcohol use and experiential related information. Chapters 4 to 6 are organized around the cognitive (knowledge) area, and Chapters 7 to 9 center on the affective domain. Appendix A contains the Alcohol Behavior Inventory, and Appendix B, review questions for use in alcohol programs.

Alcohol education research is replete with studies indicating that information alone does not improve drinking behavior. However, some essential information is needed to reinforce experiential and affective concepts. Thus this text is *not* designed to be informationally comprehensive, but to provide the basic knowledge needed to be informed about alcohol and make decisions regarding personal drinking behavior.

Darwin Dennison
Thomas Prevet
Michael Affleck

CONTENTS

Part I
EXPERIENTIAL PHASE

1 The activated approach, 3

Activated health education: theory and principles, 3
Intervention strategy, 8
Evaluation, 8
Related research, 9
Summary, 10

2 The population in question, 11

Definitions, 11
Drinking practices among the general population, 12
Drinking practices among adolescents, 13
Drinking practices among college students, 15
Drinking practices among ethnic groups, 16
Drinking practices among blacks, 17
Drinking practices among women, 17
Abstainers, 18
Summary, 19

3 Disruptive behaviors, 21

Criminal activity, 21
Student problems, 21
Automobile accidents, 23
Aggression, 23
Summary, 25

Part II
COGNITIVE PHASE

4 The disease process, 31

Health status continuum, 31
Alcohol abuse and the health continuum, 34
Summary, 36

5 Biological dimension, 39

Properties, 39
Alcoholic beverages, 40
Alcohol absorption, 41
Distribution, 43
Blood alcohol concentration, 43
Effects of alcohol, 45
Metabolism, 47
Effects on specific organs or functions, 49
Summary, 54

6 Experimental evidence, 57

Mood and aggression, 58
Relaxation, 59
Visual and auditory perception, 60
Psychomotor performance and cognitive performance, 62
Reaction and choice reaction time, 65
Driving, 67
Accidents, 69
Alcohol and perception, 72
Alcohol and driving skills, 72
Summary, 73

ix

Part III
AFFECTIVE PHASE

7 Affective domain, 77

Procedures, 80
Principles, 81
Summary, 83

8 Psychosocial components, 85

Self-concept, 86
Alienation, 88
Peer group pressure, 88
Dominance, 89
Psychological needs, 90

9 Group activities, 93

More than hello exercise, 93
First impressions exercise, 94
Alcohol education relevancy exercise, 95
Alcohol concern exercise, 95
"Feelings" word description exercise, 96
Games people play exercise, 97
Social drinking situations exercise, 101
Drinking behavior continuum, 102
Ideal vs. real drinking behavior, 103
Alcohol commitment activity, 103
Affective evaluation activity, 103
Summary, 107

Appendixes

A Alcohol behavior inventory, 110

B Review tests (cognitive information), 117

Part I

EXPERIENTIAL PHASE

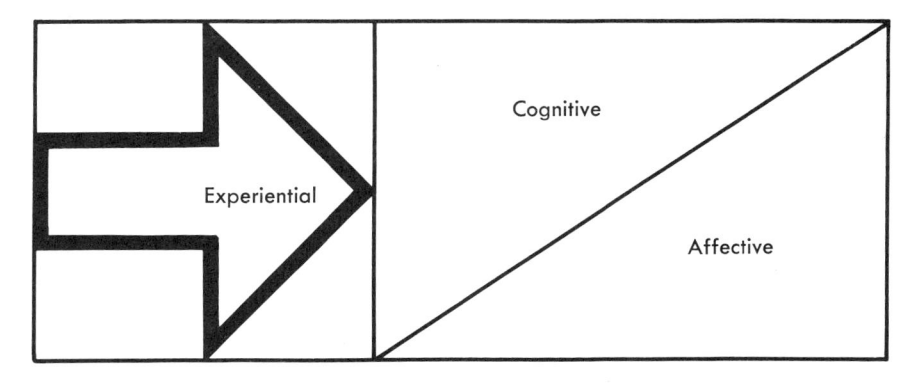

Schema for activated health education.

1 THE ACTIVATED APPROACH

Traditionally, formal education is a passive process. The providers of service (educators) lecture and the consumers of education (students) take notes. The providers make assignments and the consumers write papers and take tests. These are passive tasks, in which there is very little, if any, interaction with subject matter reality.

The practice of medicine and the delivery of health care are also passive processes. The providers of health care (physicians) prescribe treatment and the consumers of health services (patients) take medications. The providers examine, analyze, and recommend, and the consumers are expected to comply. These passive tasks communicate only minimal understanding of the disease process and the role of individual behavior in illness.

These simplified examples give the basic rationale for establishing an active partnership between the providers of health care and the consumers of health services. When this partnership has meaningful interaction, there is improved individual health behavior. An important role of health education is to facilitate an active partnership between providers and consumers.

Activated health education was designed to stimulate the partnership. In this process, health educators involve the consumers directly with the issues and problems of the disease process. Health educators communicate the importance of individual health behavior in the disease process. To accomplish this, health educators integrate content with specific events. Activated health education emphasizes consumer and provider involvement.

In alcohol education programs the health educator is the facilitator who designs and directs events. The *providers* are members of the service community that deal with alcohol problems, including police, attorneys, counselors, physicians, and psychiatrists. The *consumers* are those individuals participating in alcohol-related programs of prevention, treatment, and rehabilitation. These programs may be based in a hospital, a church, a community agency, a university, or wherever. The *health educator* is primarily involved in programs of prevention with the major aim of instilling responsible drinking behaviors by linking provider and consumer activity.

■ ACTIVATED HEALTH EDUCATION: THEORY AND PRINCIPLES

Research literature that reported programs of improved health behavior was reviewed and analyzed to determine the best way of increasing provider and consumer involvement. Basic principles from these programs were identified and then, with modifications, applied to an instructional model. Common program procedures related to improve health behavior were also adapted to the model. After a careful analysis of the principles and procedures of the model, it seemed that if health education programs were going to modify behavior, the program consumers must be activated and the providers must be involved in the process. This is the underlying theory of activated health education.

Consumers are taught to become *active* in their own health maintenance through laboratory exercises, field study, organized discussion, and other activity. Consumers are made *aware* or the various influences on their health; they learn to measure and evaluate their own health. The consumers are *responsible* for devising and implementing their own program of health maintenance with assistance from health educators. Active, aware, and responsible are the basic principles of activated health education.

Activated health education uses a standardized instructional model that corresponds to the principles devised from the research. The instructional model has three phases: an experiential phase, a cognitive phase, and an affective phase. The cognitive phase is gradually diminished because knowledge by itself does not change health behavior. However, as research cited later in this chapter indicates, knowledge preceded by experience and followed by use does effect positive health behavior. The affective phase increases in duration and follows the other phases to help people incorporate the new health behaviors and responsibility for these behaviors into their lives.

☐ **Experiential phase**

The experiential phase consists of field and laboratory activity. In this phase, consumers in programs learn to be aware of their physical and behavioral health, measure their physiological health and evaluate their behavioral health, and assess positive and negative influences on their health. The experiential phase initiates the activation process so consumers can discover the limits of their health and the scope of health concerns.

Field activity. The first part of the experiential phase in alcohol education includes field activity. The field activity is organized to provide the consumers with the opportunity to observe community activities and programs related to alcohol abuse. The activity should be designed to allow the consumers to gain first-hand experience regarding alcohol problems and the roles of providers (Table 1).

The best experience is direct provider-consumer exchange. For example, it would be ideal for the consumers individually to accompany police on late night weekend patrols. But this might not be possible because of administrative factors. Thus the next best situation would be to have a police officer describe recent alcohol-related arrests and problems to the consumers during the activated health education program.

These field experiences provide the consumers with information regarding the extent of alcohol abuse and how alcohol problems interface with all aspects of community life. The experiences acquaint the consumers with ramifications of alcohol at the extreme end of the drinking continuum. Consumers, after participating in field activity, indicate that these experiences have lasting impact on them, and many consumers have indicated that these experiences have modified their personal drinking behavior.

Table 1. Suggested field activities and objectives

Activity	Objective
Accompany police on late night weekend patrols.	Provides observer with relationship of alcohol problems to community turmoil including auto accidents, fights, vandalism, domestic arguments, and rape.
Visit court sessions related to driving while intoxicated (DWI) and other alcohol related offenses.	Acquaints observer with complexities of legal-judicial system and problems of enforcement and conviction.
Attend Alcoholics Anonymous and other community-based programs for alcoholics and their families.	Allows observer to listen to dialogue of alcoholics regarding psychosocial problems related to alcoholism and difficulties they experience.
Tour treatment hospitals or detoxification centers or both.	Assists observer in understanding principles of treatment procedures and physiological problems that accompany alcoholism.
Visit halfway houses and rehabilitation centers.	In some instances counselors will organize programs so that observers may interact with alcoholics regarding nonalcoholic related concerns.
Attend Court School for Problem Drinkers (these programs are designed for first and second offenders in lieu of imprisonment or fines or both).	Provides observer with information regarding secondary and tertiary prevention efforts.

If a consumer or group of consumers has drinking problems, it is recommended that the full complement of suggested field activities be included in the program. However, consumers without drinking problems would experience only a few of the field activities. However, each consumer should have the opportunity to interact with individuals who have experienced the other field activities. Research isolating the effect of field activity on self-reported drinking behavior has shown that the activity is a critical part of the program. Thus every effort should be made to include as many field activities in the program as possible.

The suggested field activities are merely suggestions. Each health educator must use activities related to convenience, time allotment, scheduling factors, and the availability of these types of experiences in their community. In some instances consumers will suggest other meaningful field experiences to replace a planned activity.

Other field activities are innumerable. For example, the consumers might interview key provider personnel of any community prevention, rehabilitation, or treatment program. The consumers also might interview clientele of these programs. Consumers who have an acquaintance or friend with an alcohol-related problem might schedule an informal interview regarding the general aspects of their condition. In addition, there may be opportunities for consumers to directly observe specific drinking activity at a bar or party for insights and relationships.

All field activities used must be clearly defined as to the function and procedures that would be followed. The consumer should detail what type of information would be sought and how it would be organized and used. Health educators must clear with their administrators *all* activities for compliance with local and human subjects standards. The function of the experiential phase is to provide first-hand knowledge; therefore any field activity that meets this criteria should be encouraged.

Laboratory aspect. The laboratory aspect of the experiential phase allows an opportunity for the consumer to assess the physiological effects of alcohol on his or her own behavior. Laboratory activity requires special equipment and strict adherence to formal laboratory protocol. The specific function of the laboratory activity is to provide first-hand experience of the effects of low concentrations of alcohol on the consumer's memory, coordination, and relaxation mechanisms (Table 2).

As a standard part of health education practice, all laboratory experience must be cleared by local human subjects committees. Laboratory experiences must be on a voluntary basis with appropriate alternatives for those individuals who do not wish to participate. During laboratory experiences, consumers ingesting alcohol must be of the legal drinking age and must have given consent to participate. Never should the blood alcohol concentration of 0.075 be exceeded. Consumers taking medications contraindicated with alcohol should not participate. And, as a final precaution, a physician or nurse should be in attendance during the laboratory experience.

Laboratory and field experiences are administratively complex to operationalize. However, these experiences are critical to the activation process. Experience has shown that laboratory and field experiences are an important and critical dimension of a suc-

Table 2. Suggested laboratory activity and objectives

Activity	Objective
Breath testers—estimate blood alcohol levels	Enables observer to relate subjective experience to actual BAC
Simple and multiple reaction time instruments	Provides observer with direct experience in regard to effect of moderate alcohol levels on reaction time
Tachistoscopes	
Visual perception	Allows observer to experience changes in visual perception (i.e., rapidly displayed numbers and letters)
Cognitive process	Acquaints observer with effects of alcohol on over-learned tasks (i.e., naming numbers)
Electromyographs (EMG)	Aids observer in understanding of relationship between muscle tension and moderate blood alcohol levels
Hand precision instruments	Assist observer in correlating effect of alcohol on eye-hand coordination

cessful program. Laboratory experiences improve the probability of responsible drinking behavior of the consumers and thus are worth the time and effort.

☐ Cognitive phase

The cognitive phase presents the important information of the health area to the consumers. This phase includes the rationale for laboratory and field experience as well as general evidence about the relationship between an individual's health behavior and general health. Information related to physiological functioning and the evaluation of an individual's personal susceptibility to health behavior conditions is also included in this phase.

The cognitive phase of alcohol education is detailed in Chapters 4 through 6. These chapters explain the relationship of alcohol to health status, the pharmacological properties and effects of alcohol, and the experimental research related to alcohol use. Information related to the disease concept as it relates to alcohol abuse, the physiological effects of alcohol at different blood alcohol concentrations, the absorption and oxidation of alcohol in the body, and the concepts of physical dependence and tolerance are included.

The experimental research presented in Chapter 6 is the conclusion of the cognitive phase. The underlying theory of this phase is that quality empirical research presented objectively to the consumers will create cognitive dissonance and individual susceptibility to alcohol-related problems. More specifically, individuals who drink are, in essence, taking a risk. The more an individual drinks, in frequency and amount, the greater the risk. The evidence included in this chapter explains how moderate amounts of alcohol ingestion affect various dimension of our lives. Mood levels, visual perception, psychomotor performance, and other factors are presented to assist individuals with the important information regarding alcohol use and its effect on their daily lives.

☐ Affective phase

During the affective phase the consumers identify and clarify their personal health values through discussion. Their actual and ideal health behaviors are discussed. Before completion of this phase, the health educator helps the consumers establish their own programs of health maintenance based on their own values. The health educator's responsibilities are to activate the consumers, make them aware of the influences of their health, and help the consumer establish a health maintenance program. The consumers' responsibility is to implement or ignore their programs of health maintenance. If the activated health education program is organized and presented adequately, a significant number of consumers will continue their newly established programs. The net effect is improved health behavior.

During the affective phase of alcohol education, activities are initiated for a few minutes at the end of each class and increased in time allotment with each class. These activities eventually occupy most of the class period. Consumers are organized into small groups to experience the affective activities. These activities are designed to generate honest reactions and feelings about drinking behavior and alcohol-related behavior. Values are identified and clarified. Consumers are asked to make personal value commitments to themselves and their group regarding the type of behavior they would adhere to during and after the class regarding the use of alcohol. These affective activities are designed to improve alcohol-related behavior and to motivate the consumers to apply behaviors after the instructional process.

Chapters 7 through 9 detail the specifics of the affective phase of alcohol education. Examples of activities are outlined in Chapter 9. Chapters 7 and 8 present the rationale and importance of these procedures and how they are related to alcohol education.

■ INTERVENTION STRATEGY

Instructional methodology used within activated health education must reflect the specific consumer group (children, adults, patients) and consumer base (elementary or secondary school, outpatient clinic, volunteer group). In order for the activated process to be successful, the health educator must organize detailed protocol for the specific consumer group and base.

The experiential phase is health educator dominated. The consumer follows an established procedure of experiences and activities that are highly organized. The health educator directs the activities so the consumers experience various aspects of the measurement of their physiological and behavioral health in the laboratory and scope of alcohol-related concerns in the field. The experiential phase is formal and goal directed.

The cognitive phase is health educator–consumer oriented. Interaction between the health educator and consumers increases during this phase. The instructional climate is less formal. Requested and planned information is presented.

The affective phase is consumer centered. The health educator becomes a facilitator who helps consumers identify their own health values. Various learning games, organized discussion, role playing, and other activities are used in this phase. The affective phase is not evaluated in terms of consumer behavior. The instructional climate is informal.

Generally the experiential phase makes the consumers *active* in situations related to alcohol use and abuse. The cognitive phase makes the consumers *aware* of the influences of alcohol on their lives and the lives of individuals in their community. The affective phase assists the consumers in making *responsible* decisions about their own drinking behaviors.

■ EVALUATION

An important factor of activated health education is to provide an internal and external evaluation system. Internal evaluation provides the health educator with immediate feedback regarding the completion, success, and acceptance of the program. For example, in the experiential phase the consumers either pass by completing the procedures and activities (Tables 1 and 2) or are given an incomplete until the tasks are finished. The health educator would merely design a check-off list for the selected activities. In the cognitive phase, objective tests are used to determine if the consumer has learned the information deemed important and necessary (see examples in Appendix B). Alternate form tests are used so that the evaluation is based on established competencies and not achieved knowledge at a specific time. In the affective phase, questionnaires are used to provide the health educator with information about the selected activities, but the consumers are not evaluated. A discussion of this procedure is found on p. 103, and two examples of affective questionnaires are included on pp. 104 and 106. These questionnaires determine the success of the activities and whether the health educator is facilitating such success.

External evaluation is designed for program comparisons. The Alcohol Behavior Inventory (Appendix A), in which consumers report their alcohol usage behavior over a specific period of time, provides data regarding dangerous and disruptive behaviors. This inventory was deemed valid and reliable. Reliability and validity of the Alcohol Behavior Inventory are discussed on p. 113. Inventory data can be used to determine the effectiveness of programs and compare variables within a program. In this manner, a base of successful activities can be obtained for the primary prevention of alcohol problems.

■ RELATED RESEARCH

The principles of activated health education have been evaluated and have advanced the behavioral study of alcohol education. Research has provided numerous successful efforts in changing attitudes and cognitive information. However, only three educational programs reported in the literature that produce behavioral change used experimental procedures that could be replicated. Two of these programs were organized around the activated health education model and have similar components.

The first study examined the knowledge level, attitudes, and drinking behaviors of 97 experimental and 80 control subjects involved in an alcohol education study in a high school in the suburbs of Boston.[1] In this study the experimental group was exposed to a 1-week alcohol education program designed around small group discussion. The control group was also exposed to the same small group format; however, their discussions were concerned with current social issues rather than alcohol use. Both groups were asked to complete a questionnaire about drinking at the beginning and end of the program and again one year later. The results of the study showed that an intensive alcohol education program can positively change attitudes, cause significant changes in knowledge about alcohol, and affect behavior. The researchers found in a posttest of the subjects a year after the program that there was a strong tendency for the experimental subjects to become intoxicated less often than the controls. It appeared that the program of small group discussion was successful in discouraging teenagers from becoming intoxicated.

The second study investigated the effects of alcohol-related field experiences on the drinking behavior of university students.[2] In this study students in the experimental group were required to participate in selected alcohol-related field activities, whereas the students in the control group were not required to participate in these activities. Some of these activities included accompanying police on weekend patrols and visiting with patients in alcohol rehabilitation programs. The same instructor and standardized instructional procedures were used with both groups. This experimental design isolated the effects of the field experiences on the drinking behavior of the university students. Through the use of an anonymous self-report inventory to assess drinking behavior, a significant difference was found in the frequency of perceived intoxication when the inventories of the experimental and control groups were compared. Students in the experimental groups who had participated in the field experiences had a lower utilization of automobiles during and after drinking.

The third study was conducted at State University of New York at Buffalo with undergraduate students enrolled in a health education course.[3] The study determined the effects of an activated alcohol education program on self-reported drinking behavior. The effectiveness of the activation program was evaluated by an alcohol behavior inventory that was administered to experimental and control groups before, immediately after, and one month following the program presentation. Findings indicated that activated alcohol education significantly reduced dangerous and disruptive behaviors related to alcohol use.

A one-year follow-up study of this program was conducted.[4] Sixty-six percent of the experimental group and 73% of the control group returned an alcohol behavior inventory. Significant differences in drinking severity were found between groups. The group that participated in the program drank significantly less than those who were not exposed to the program.

■ SUMMARY

This chapter described the rationale and reasoning for use of the activated health education approach. The basic principles and program components were detailed. Experiential phase activities, including the field and laboratory, were presented. Research on the effects of alcohol education programs utilizing the activated approach was cited.

REFERENCES

1. Williams, A. F., Dicco, L. M., and Unterberger, H.: Philosophy and evaluation of an alcohol education program, Q. J. Stud. Alcohol **29**:685-702, 1968.
2. Dennison, D.: The effects of selected field experiences upon the drinking behavior of university students, J. Sch. Health **44**:16-24, 1974.
3. Prevet, T. E.: The effects of an alcohol instructional model on self-reported drinking behavior of university students, Unpublished doctoral dissertation, State University of New York at Buffalo, May 1977.
4. Affleck, B.: The effects of an alcohol instructional model on self-reported drinking behavior of university students: one year later, Unpublished masters project, State University of New York at Buffalo, May 1978.

2 THE POPULATION IN QUESTION

The focus of this chapter is on who drinks and how much. The first section of the chapter provides definitions of the terms related to the frequency and occasions of drinking. The following sections detail the recent studies regarding alcohol use incidence and prevalence. The chapter establishes baseline data regarding the frequency and amount of drinking among various individuals and groups. The important variables thought to influence or effect drinking are identified.

■ DEFINITIONS

To assist in the analysis of alcohol usage a drinking classification system is presented. Studies of alcohol usage vary because of the differences among design and instrumentation. For these reasons this chapter will present compilations of studies as they relate to this specific classification system. Whenever possible, the following terminology will be used to standardize references to drinking behavior. Five drinking classifications will be used including heavy drinking, moderate drinking, light drinking, infrequent drinking, and abstinence. The concept for this system was adapted from an instrument originally developed by the Social Research Group, George Washington University, Washington, D.C. (Table 3).

Heavy drinkers are those individuals who drink three or more times a day regardless of the amount or who drink two or three times per month but almost always have five or more drinks. Heavy drinkers may never become alcoholics. *Moderate drinkers* are individuals who drink twice a day, one or two drinks most of the time. *Light drinkers* drink only one or two drinks daily or five or six drinks once a month. *Infrequent drinkers* drink less than once a month but at least once a year. *Abstainers* drink less than once a year or not at all.

Problem drinking occurs when drinking causes physical, psychological, or social harm to the drinker or others. Problem drinking manifests itself in the form of dangerous or disruptive behaviors that occur during, after, and as a result of drinking. Some of these behaviors may include legal complications, domestic quarrels, and personal conflict. During an individual's lifetime problem drinking may occur infrequently or repetitively. Problem drinking may or may not lead to alcoholism.

Blood alcohol concentration (BAC) is the ratio of the amount of alcohol to total blood volume. As an example, in an average male, one drink would produce a BAC of approximately 0.02 (2 parts of alcohol to every 100 parts of blood). At the 0.07 level, an individual is considered *impaired* and at the 0.1 level an individual would be considered *intoxicated*.

Table 3. Classification system of drinking behavior

Frequency of drinking	Number of drinks		
	5+	3-4	1-2
3 times/day	H*	H	H
2 times/day	H	H	M
1 times/day	H	H/M	L
3-4 times/week	H	M	L
1-2 times/week	H	M	L
2-3 times/month	H	M/L	L
1 times/month	M	L	L

*H, heavy; M, moderate; L, light.

		Heavy	Abstain
Men	73%	21%	23%
Women	49%	5%	40%

Fig. 1. Drinking practices among adults.

■ DRINKING PRACTICES AMONG THE GENERAL POPULATION

A national study of drinking practices was conducted by Calahan and will be referred to as American Drinking Practices (ADP).[1] Harris and Associates, Inc., conducted two national surveys on separate occasions. Gallup also surveyed the nation's drinking practices.

The ADP determined that 68% of the adult population drinks. The Gallup poll indicated that 65% of adult Americans drink. The first Harris survey[2] further substantiated these data and reported that 76% of adults between the ages of 18 and 29, 71% between the ages of 30 and 49, 58% between the ages of 50 and 64, and 45% over age 65 drank.

The second survey conducted by Harris[3] asked questions related to attitudes and drinking behavior. Approximately 73% of the men and 49% of the women identified themselves as drinkers. In the eastern United States 71% of the population were identified as drinkers, whereas in the South only 41% of the population were identified as drinkers (Fig. 1).

The ADP results were classified as follows: 15% infrequent drinkers, 28% light drinkers, 13% moderate drinkers, and 12% heavy drinkers. More men were classified as heavy drinkers (21%) than women (5%), and more women were abstainers (40%) than men (23%). Harris and Gallup did not collect data related to drinking classifications (Fig. 2).

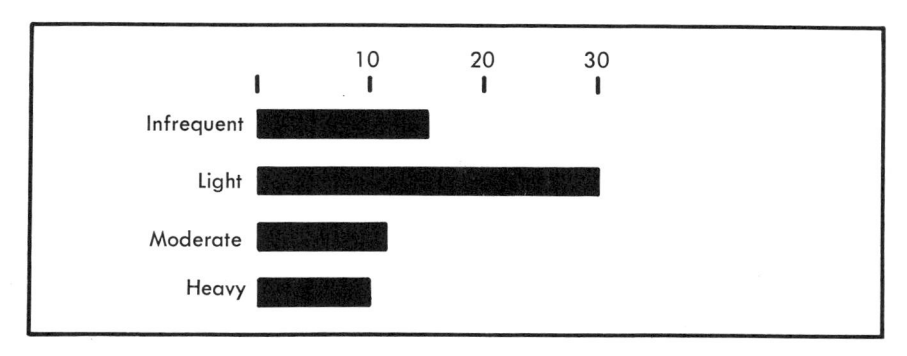

Fig. 2. Adult drinking patterns.

■ DRINKING PRACTICES AMONG ADOLESCENTS

Alcohol is the most widely used drug among adolescents in the United States. Acording to a comprehensive study[4] of the extent of illicit drug use among high school adolescents, the percentage of students reporting having tried alcohol ranged from 32% in the seventh grade to 77% in the twelfth grade. Heavy drinking was reported by 1% of the seventh grade students and 4% of the twelfth graders. Peers were often cited as being the source of alcohol.

A study of similar magnitude and with comparable results was conducted in Anchorage, Alaska.[5] Once again alcohol was the most commonly used drug at all grade levels. The analysis of data indicated that 42% of the 15,000 students reported using alcohol ten or more times in the past and 23% reported light or moderate drinking during the week of the survey.

Another large study[6] of the drinking attitudes and behavior of 19,000 students in grades seven through twelve was conducted in Kentucky. In this study 3% were classified as heavy drinkers, 8% as moderate drinkers, 18% as light drinkers, 26% as infrequent drinkers, and 45% as abstainers. Half of the drinkers generally consumed beer, while 34% drank wine, and 15%, distilled spirits. Of the drinkers, 45% reported usually drinking less than two drinks when they drank. Twenty percent reported drinking up to six drinks, while 34% usually had more than six drinks (Fig. 3).

When the drinking practices of high school students were examined in two communities where abstinence was the norm, the study[7] revealed that fewer students drink in an abstinence setting than elsewhere. Of the 639 students surveyed, 47% of the male students and 20% of the female students were classified as drinkers. However, of those students who did drink, a high percentage of problem drinkers was noted. Thirty percent of the male students and 7% of the female students were found to be problem drinkers. The risk in the pattern of alcohol use tends to be greater when drinking is done under conditions of illegality.

In another study[8] high school students located in a lower-middle- and middle-class

```
                    10    20    30    40
Abstainers  ███████████████████████████████
Infrequent  ██████████████
Light       ████████
Moderate    ████
Heavy       ██
```

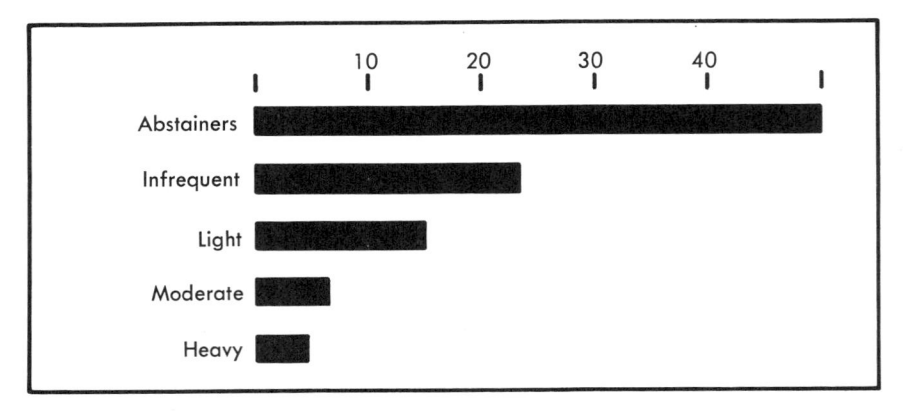

Fig. 3. Drinking practices among high school students.

semi-industrial city were compared to students living in a middle- and upper-middle-class residential town. The findings revealed that 66% of the senior students in the city and 44% in the residential town were heavy drinkers. Among the junior high students the percentage of heavy drinkers were found to be 33% and 18%, respectively. At the senior high level no difference in alcohol use was found between male and female students. However, in the junior high school, boys reported being heavier drinkers than the girls.

A greater frequency of alcohol use was found among the illicit drug user than the nonuser. A study[9] that explored the relationship between alcohol use and the use of illicit drugs among high school students revealed that the illicit drug user uses alcohol more frequently than does the drug abstainer. From the study it was postulated that it is easier for students who participate in one prohibited behavior to participate in other similar prohibitive behaviors.

Adolescent drug use begins with alcohol, according to a study conducted in New York State.[10] When the patterns of multiple drug use of a sample of over 8,000 public secondary school students were examined, the descriptive data reported that 82% of the students drank beer or wine and 65% used distilled spirits. This pattern of drug use was found to correlate with the use of other illicit drugs. The study concluded that the concern over drug use should focus on all drugs and should not be restricted solely to the use of illicit drugs.

Student use of alcohol increase after graduation from high school. A national longitudinal study of public high school students concerning their drug use during and after high school showed that 81% of the students used alcoholic beverages during the high school years. Thirty-three percent were found to use alcohol weekly. In the year after graduation from high school the percentage of alcohol use increased to 89% and 44%, respectively.[11]

Similar rates of increase in drug use were reported in another short-term longitudinal study. This study was conducted on a representative sample of New York State public secondary school students in the fall of 1971 and the spring of 1972. Over the year the students reported slight increases in drug use. The largest increase was seen in the use of hard liquor (6%). Despite the short time period between the presurvey and postsurvey, the study clearly demonstrated that alcohol usage increases during adolescence.[12]

■ DRINKING PRACTICES AMONG COLLEGE STUDENTS

Alcohol is the most widely used mood-modifying drug on college campuses. A comprehensive study of drug use behavior of undergraduate students at five American universities was conducted. The percentages of use among students at these five universities ranged from 78% to 92%.[13]

At the conclusion of an extensive study on drug use among college students, alcohol was found to be the most frequently used substance and specific characteristics of the drinker were identified.

The drug patterns of 24,609 students in the university system of Georgia showed that 46% of the students drank. The students with the highest frequency of drinking were found to be over 23 years of age, white, divorced, and claimed no affiliation with any religious denomination.[14]

In a longitudinal study of drugs on a California university campus, virtually all the students indicated they used alcohol at one time or another. Most students revealed thay had tried beer or wine. The intake frequency of all forms of alcohol increased with seniority.[15]

The incidence of drinking was highest among senior male students from high-income families who resided in urban areas. Their parents were well educated and also drank. These data were obtained from a survey of students from 37 colleges and universities throughout the United States.[16]

The percentage of college students reporting frequent drinking was found to be highest in those students residing off campus. This information was generated in a study at Oregon University. The questionnaire revealed that 95% of the students surveyed had at some time consumed alcohol. Of the students still drinking at the time of the survey, 68% used distilled spirits while 76% drank either beer or wine. The students living off campus or with fraternity groups were found to drink, beer and wine more frequently (three to ten times weekly) than the students living in cooperative housing and dormitories. The same was found for the frequency of hard liquor use [17] (Fig. 4).

The drinking practices of students at a southern university[18] were analyzed according to the demographic information obtained. The analysis of the senior student responses to the questionnaire indicated that 85% of the men and 82% of the women were drinkers. A greater percentage of students from cities were found to be drinkers than students from small towns or rural areas. A relationship between drinking and family income was also found. Students from families with high income drank more

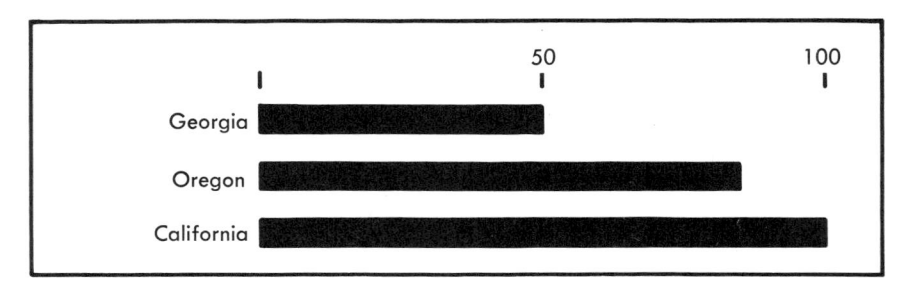

Fig. 4. Drinking practices among college students.

than students from low-income families. The incidence of drinking also increased in direct proportion to the increase in the educational level of both parents. The percentage of seniors reported as drinkers also depended on the drinking habits of the parents. In general, the highest percentage in the incidence of drinking was reported by students whose parents were classified as heavy drinkers.

■ DRINKING PRACTICES AMONG ETHNIC GROUPS

Early studies in the United States have indicated that ethnic characteristics are associated with drinking behavior. A high prevalence of drinking was reported among Italians in the United States, but they experienced relatively low rates of alcoholism.[19] Irish Americans were found to have high incidences of problem drinking and alcohol use.[20]

In the ADP study, 93% of the Irish group were drinkers, followed by the Italians (91%), English (89%), Polish (85%), and Germans (85%). Heavy drinking proportions were Irish (31%), English (24%), Italians (19%), Polish (14%), and Germans (13%). Heavier drinking occurred more when a person's father was foreign born than when one's father was born in the United States.

In the Western New York survey of drinking practices, no conclusive evidence was observed "that ethnic origin or national identity play a major role in determining drinking behavior."[21] Heavy drinking among the Irish group (27%) was very close to that in the United Kingdom (25%), German (25%), Poland (24%), and Italy (18%). Individuals claiming the United States as their country of origin had a heavy drinking rate of 22%. Drinking prevalence was virtually the same for all groups: Irish (90%), Italian (90%), Germans (88%), English (87%), Polish (84%), and Americans (84%) (Fig. 5).

The early studies did not factor out the function of age in relation to drinking. This made ethnic groups with younger age proportions appear to be heavier drinkers. At this time, overall drinking classifications among ethnic groups appear to be balancing. As immigrants are assimilated into the culture, fewer drinking behavior differences can be found that are related to ethnicity.

	ADP	WNY
Irish	31	27
Italians	24	18
English	19	25
Polish	14	24
Germans	13	25

Fig. 5. HEAVY drinking practices among ethnic groups.

	Black	White
Light/moderate	36	42
Heavy	14	12

Fig. 6. Drinking practices among black and white women.

■ DRINKING PRACTICES AMONG BLACKS

In a summary of studies related to alcohol and blacks, the limited literature suggested that their drinking behavior was different than that of whites.[22] Drinking was found to be twice as common among urban black men when compared to a similar sample of white men.[22] In another study, 84% of the blacks had begun drinking before age 19, and the author suggested that the black culture may have a greater permissiveness for early drinking.[22] Black alcoholism rates were reported to be substantially higher than white rates.[22] These observations, however, were postulated to be due to higher percentages of blacks who were unmarried, divorced, or separated in the sample than whites.

The ADP study reported no differences between black and white persons' drinking behavior when the total sample was observed. In the light and moderate drinking classifications, 36% were black and 42% white. In the heavy drinking classifications, 14% were black and 12% white. Black women had a higher proportion of abstainers (51% vs. 39%) and a higher rate of heavy drinkers (11% vs. 4%) (Fig. 6).

■ DRINKING PRACTICES AMONG WOMEN

Many individuals consider alcohol problems to be a "man's illness." But authorities indicate that women are less likely to seek help and are better able to mask the symptoms of problem drinking than men. Dr. Marvin Block, former chairman of the American Medical Association Committee on Alcoholism, estimates that approximately 5 million women in the United States today are experiencing some type of alcohol problem.

Previously cited data indicate that women drink less than their male counterparts at all ages and in most milieus. However, anecdotal literature suggests that when women become problem drinkers, they differ from men on several important dimensions. Specifically, the woman has been described as a solitary drinker who consumes fewer drinks but drinks more frequently than her male counterpart.[23] The heavy-drinking woman is more likely to have sexual problems[24] and depressive disorders.[25] Thus the progression to alcoholism is more rapid and severe than with men.[26] Sociological ramifications tend to make women generally less receptive to alcohol rehabilitative methods.

During pregnancy, women report a reduced amount of drinking.[27] The major reason cited by the women for the reduced drinking was adverse physiological effects including nausea, stomach irritation, headaches, and the diuretic effects of alcohol. The authors hypothesize the alcohol is an embryotoxin, and the natural rejection of alcohol may be a biological regulation to substances that are potentially noxious to the fetus.

Treatment and rehabilitation facilities are reported to be grossly inadequate for women. In some institutions, facilities are provided for men only.[28] This situation is postulated to be related to women alcoholics being diagnosed and treated at later stages than men alcoholics. Thus alcoholism among women tends to be more acute and the problems related to it compounded.

ABSTAINERS

Abstainers represent an extreme end of a drinking continuum. Previously cited data indicated that between 14% and 32% of the population are abstainers. Most abstainers indicated they were lifetime abstainers, but approximately 30% indicated they were drinkers at some earlier time in their lives.[29] In a society where moderate drinking is considered the norm, these individuals may be regarded as a deviant minority.

Abstainers reported that they had a close friend or relative with a drinking problem.[29] In addition, they were more likely to report that drinking does more harm than good and that nothing good can be said about drinking. Abstainers, as would seem likely, have family backgrounds that disapprove of drinking.

Women at all age groups and milieus are more likely to be abstainers than men. The female abstainer's personality was described as "unquestioning and uncomplaining inferiority."[30] Women problem drinkers and abstainers were found to have common negative personality traits including self-defeatism, pessimism, withdrawal, and feelings of guilt. However, the abstaining women were judged to be conventional, ethical, and emotionally controlled.

Among high school students, abstainers personally disapproved of drinking. The attended church regularly and were better informed regarding the depressant effects and the nonnutritive value of alcohol. The high school abstainers thought that only a minority of their friends were drinkers.[6]

■ SUMMARY

Alcohol is the favorite drug of American society. It is used and misused by more people than any other harmful substance among the general society; however, approximately 50% of the United States population drink only infrequently or lightly. Alcohol is used most often in the eastern United States and by men.

Alcohol use by adolescents and college students increases with age and social class. That is, the older the individual and the higher in social class, the more likely the adolescent and college student will drink. Adolescent alcohol use is most often a condition of illegality, whereas college student alcohol use is reported to be an integral part of the social scene.

Heavy drinking, once thought to be related to ethnic background, is now regarded as being related to the younger age of new immigrants. Also, many new immigrants are separated from tradition and family ties, which is thought to be related to increased drinking. Heavy drinking differences among ethnic groups cannot be identified, as these groups are assimilated into general society.

Blacks show no differences in drinking practices from whites when social class and familial turmoil are comparable.

At all ages and social classes, women use alcohol less than do men. Alcohol may be naturally rejected by pregnant women because of the potential harm to the fetus. Alcohol problems among women tend to be more debilitating because relatives and friends view the condition as a personal weakness, whereas alcohol problems in men are more likely to be viewed as a disease. Treatment and rehabilitation facilities for women are often minimal.

REFERENCES

1. Calahan, D., Cisin, I. H., and Crossley, H. M.: American drinking practices, monograph no. 6, Rutgers Center of Alcohol Studies, New Brunswick, N.J., 1969, Journal of Studies on Alcohol, Inc.
2. Harris, L., and Associates, Inc.: American attitudes toward alcohol and alcoholics, study no.2128, Report prepared for the NIAAA, Rockville, Md., 1971, National Institute on Alcohol Abuse and Alcoholism.
3. Harris, L., and Associates, Inc.: Public awareness and the NIAAA advertising campaign and public attitudes toward drinking and alcohol abuse, PB-244 147, Springfield, Va., 1974, National Technical Information Service.
4. Gossett, J. T., Lewis, J. M., and Phillips, V. A.: Extent and prevalence of illicit drug use as reported by 56,745 students, J.A.M.A. **261:**1464-1470, 1971.
5. Porter, M., et al.: Drug use in Anchorage, Alaska, J.A.M.A. **223:**657-664, 1973.
6. Kane, R. L., and Patterson, E.: Drinking attitudes and behaviors of high school students in Kentucky, J. Stud. Alcohol **33:**635-646, 1972.
7. Globetti, G: The use of beverage alcohol by youth in an abstinence setting, J. Sch. Health **39:**179-183, 1969.

8. Wechsler, H., and Thum, D.; Teenage drinking, drug use and social correlates, J. Stud. Alcohol **34:**1220-1227, 1973.
9. Shapiro, R. D.: Alcohol, tobacco and illicit drug use amont adolescents, Int. J. Addict. **10:**387-390, 1975.
10. Single, E., Kandel, D., and Faust, R.: Patterns of multiple drug use in high school, J. Health Soc. Behav. **15:**344-357, 1974.
11. Johnson, L. D.: Drug use during and after high school: results of a national longitudinal study, Am J. Public Health **64:**29-37,1974.
12. Kandel, D., Single, E., and Kessler, R.: The epidemiology of drug use among New York State high school students: distribution, trends and change in rates of use, Am. J. Public Health **66:**43-53, 1976.
13. Toohey, J. V.: An analysis of drug use behavior at five American universities, Sch. Health **41:**464-468, 1971.
14. Stimbu, J. L., and Sims, O. S.: A university system drug profile, Int. J. Addict. **9:**569-583, 1974.
15. Garfield, M., and Garfield, E.: A longitudinal study of drugs on a campus, Int. J. Addict. **8:**599-611, 1973.
16. Hanson, D. J.: Drinking attitudes and behaviors among college students, J. Alcohol Drug Educ. **19:**6-14, 1974.
17. Penn, J. R.: College student life style and frequency of alcohol usage, J. Am. Coll. Health Assoc. **22:**220-222. 1974.
18. Glassco, K.: Drinking habits of seniors in a southern university, J. Alcohol Drug Educ. **21:**25-29, 1975.
19. Lolli, G., Serianni, E., Golder, G. M., and Luzzato-Fegiz, P.: Alcohol in Italian culture: food and wine in relation to sobriety among Italians and Italian Americans, monograph no. 3, New Brunswick, N.J., 1958, Rutgers Center of Alcohol Studies.
20. Bales, R. F.: Attitudes toward drinking in the Irish culture. In Pittman, D. J., and Snyder, C. R., editors: Society, culture, and drinking patterns, New York, 1962, John Wiley & Sons.
21. Barnes, G. M.: A perspective on drinking among teenagers with specific reference to New York State studies, J. Sch. Health **45:**386-389, 1975.
22. Viamontes, J. A., and Powell, B. J.: Dermographic characteristics of black and white male alcoholics, Int. J. Addict. **9:**489-494, 1974.
23. Horn, J. L., and Wanberg, K. W.: Females are different: some difficulties in diagnosing problems of alcohol use in women, Paper presented at the First Annual Conference of the National Institute on Alcohol Abuse and Alcoholism, Washington, D.C., June 1971.
24. Schuckit, M.: Sexual disturbance in the woman alcoholic, Hum. Sex. **6:**44-65, 1972.
25. Winokur, G., Reich, T., Rimmer, J., and Pitts, F. N., Jr.: Alcoholism III: diagnosis and familial psychiatric illness in 259 alcoholic probands, Arch. Gen. Psychiatr. **23:**104-111, 1970.
26. Curlee, J. A.: Comparison of male and female patients at an alcoholism treatment center, J. Psychol. **74:**239-247, 1970.
27. Little, R. E., Schultz, F. A., and Mandell, W.: Drinking during pregnancy, J. Stud. Alcohol **37:**375-379, 1976.
28. Casado, A.: Women alcoholics: a neglected minority, Unpublished paper, Buffalo, N.Y., May 1, 1978, Trocaire College, p. 7.
29. Cisin, I. H., and Calahan, D.: Comparison of abstainers and heavy drinkers in a national survey, Psychiatr. Res. Rep. **24:**10-12, 1968.
30. Jones, M. C.: Personality antecedents and correletes of drinking patterns in women, J. Consult. Clin. Psychol. **36:**61-69, 1971.

3 DISRUPTIVE BEHAVIORS

The literature is explicit regarding the correlation of alcohol to aggressive and disruptive behavior. The greater the amount of alcohol consumed, the higher the level of aggression. Evidence indicates that the type of beverage consumed and the milieus in which it is consumed are related to the level of aggression. Alcohol has been significantly related to criminal activity, delinquency, and accidents.

■ CRIMINAL ACTIVITY

In a 1-year period approximately five million persons were arrested for alcohol-related offenses in the United States.[1] These offenses included public drunkenness, vagrancy, disturbing the peace, drunken driving, disorderly conduct, and violation of liquor laws. Alcohol-related arrests accounted for 55% of all arrests, and in some areas this percentage was higher.[2] An analysis of police reports in Muncie, Indiana, in 1974 indicated that over 85% of all "calls" on Friday and Saturday evenings were alcohol-related.[3]

Inmates of state prisons indicated that 43% were drinking at the time of the offense that resulted in their arrest.[4] In another study,[5] arrests for crimes against persons (including murder, aggravated assault, and rape) were more common among men with recent alcohol problems and records of heavy drinking than a control group of moderate and light drinkers. Other studies have found a high incidence of heavy drinking in both murderers and murder victims.[7]

Male inmates of the North Carolina prison system who had been convicted of crimes of murder and manslaughter were studied.[8] The prisoners were placed into one of three categories: nondrinkers, drinkers, and problem drinkers. The problem drinkers were more likely to have previous nonalcohol-related criminal records. The majority of the inmates (58%) were drinking at the time of their arrest; of their victims, 40% were drinking at the time of their assault.

Delinquent adolescents being held in state detention homes were compared with nondelinquent adolescents attending secondary schools. Delinquents drank more frequently and drank a greater quantity than nondelinquents. Parents or relatives offered the nondelinquents their first drink, whereas friends and other nonrelatives obtained alcohol for the delinquent. And, as was to be expected, delinquents were arrested for drinking-related offenses more often than the nondelinquents.[9]

■ STUDENT PROBLEMS

According to a report from the National Institute on Alcohol Abuse and Alcoholism, approximately 50% of all teenagers who drink indicated they have been drunk at least once. Thirty-four percent indicated that their use of alcohol has created problems with friends or police. These estimates were established from students attending school. If teenagers who were not in school were included, the percentages were expected to be much higher.

Approximately 20% of students who drank reported involvement in such behaviors as fighting, destroying property, and damaging friendships. This information was obtained from a study of the drinking practices of high school students, which was conducted in a community that strongly censured all forms of alcohol. As expected, the users of alcohol in that community scored higher on a deviant behavior index than did the nonusers.[10]

Similar types of deviant and disruptive behavior associated with the use of alcohol were seen in high school students in Kentucky.[11] As reported by a questionnaire, 3% of those students who drank reported that drinking had occasionally interfered with their school work. Eight percent of the students reported fighting or destroying property as a result of their drinking. Drinking also resulted in automobile accidents, injury, arrest, or trouble with school officials in 4% of the student population.

A strong association was observed between drinking and delinquent behavior in a study of over 1,000 junior and senior high school students.[12] The questionnaire used in the study surveyed the frequency with which high school students had been involved in various antisocial activities. These delinquent activities ranged from minor involvement with police to more serious offenses including shoplifting and property damage. The heavy drinker reported more involvement in these various delinquent activities than did moderate or light drinkers.

An unpublished study conducted by the Sheppard Foundation reported that 15% of the students surveyed were found to be involved in some sort of misbehavior following the use of alcoholic beverages (such as fighting or destruction of property).

In another study the same percentage of high school students was found to be involved in antisocial activity during drinking.[13] Fifteen percent of the students in four New York State high schools reported engaging in at least one antisocial act when drinking within the past 3 months. Fighting, destroying property, speeding, involvement in an automobile accident, trouble with police, and appearance in court for alcohol-related behavior were included in the definition of an antisocial act.

Similar results were found in a study of a western New York school district.[14] Fourteen percent of the students reported they were involved in fighting, destruction of property, and trouble with police or school authorities one or more times while drinking.

On the college level, alcohol-related behavior also represents a problem. In an Oregon State University study,[15] students referred to the university by police or other authorities for disciplinary action were frequently found to be charged with "alcohol misconduct." The students referred for drinking misconduct were involved in aggressive acts which included property damage, harassment of police and citizens, and general disruptive behavior. Freshmen students were found overrepresented in those charged for alcohol misconduct.

■ AUTOMOBILE ACCIDENTS

One of the most serious forms of alcohol-related behavior is the use of the automobile during or after drinking. Researchers consistently report that slightly above 50% of highway accidents involve drivers who had been drinking immediately prior to the accident.[16-18] Drivers responsible for the accidents had higher BACs than those not responsible.[16] These data significantly exceed the frequency with which alcohol is found in drivers using the roads at similar times and places but not involved in accidents.[19]

Other than alcohol, age was found to be a function of alcohol-related automobile accidents. Drinking-driving behavior was found to increase with age.[20] By age 20, six out of ten individuals surveyed had driven, during the past month, after drinking. At each age (18-24), nondrinkers had fewer accidents and violations than did the drinkers, and those who drove after drinking had significantly more violations.

Drivers killed in one-car accidents were found to have higher BACs than those killed in two-car accidents.[21] These drivers were more likely to be under age 30 and killed at night on a weekend. A driver with a BAC of 0.06% is estimated to have twice the probability of a driver with a 0 BAC. A driver with a BAC of 0.10% has six times more risk, and a driver with a BAC of 0.15% has twenty-five times more risk of having an accident.[22] Canadian researchers indicate that the best way to lower alcohol-related automobile accidents is to reduce mean BACs of all drivers.[23]

A Michigan study reported that over 50% of the drivers responsible for fatal traffic accidents had "serious drinking problems of a chronic nature."[24] Forty percent of the drivers were classified as alcoholics. Most of them had at least one prior arrest for drinking while intoxicated or had driven with revoked licenses. These drivers also had significantly more prior serious accidents and moving traffic violations.

■ AGGRESSION
☐ Direct observation

The evidence previously cited indicating that alcohol is correlated with aggression has been obtained through subjective evaluation and indirect information. Experimental studies have added to the understanding of this correlation by direct observation of aggression. These studies give important insight into the nature of the problem and the difficulty in conducting research in this area.

Clinical psychologists observing the direct effects of alcohol on aggression are not in complete agreement regarding the subject. However, what is certain is that when individuals did not socially interact, alcohol did not produce aggression. However, when individuals interacted with other individuals, aggression increased after alcohol was used.

Aggression was not a consequence of the pharmacological action of alcohol. Subjects were asked to provide shock to victims in an experimental study.[25,26] Shock levels delivered by individuals under the influence of alcohol to victims in another room were not affected by the consumption of alcohol.[25,26] The shock levels remained consistent before and after drinking in experimental and control subjects. Alcohol may produce

> **MYTH:** I AM FRIENDLIER WHEN I DRINK.
>
> Evidence gathered from studies concerned with alcohol use and behavior tends to prove contrary to this statement. Alcohol consumption has been found to be related to many types of aggressive behaviors. Several studies have demonstrated that men exhibit more aggressive behavior and are less friendly during and after drinking.[25,32,33] Men have also been found to be more boisterous, elated, and outwardly aggressive while drinking.[34] Their preference for aggression[35] and their thoughts about physical aggression also have been found to increase after drinking moderate amounts of alcohol.[36]
>
> Alcohol has also been shown to be present when different types of aggressive behavior occur. More than half the patients admitted to a hospital in Boston with injuries resulting from fights or assaults were found to have positive alcohol readings.[12] Heavy drinking has been found to be related to interpersonal aggressive acts such as physical assault and murder.[37] Heavy drinkers are also overrepresented in crimes related to sexual assaults, robbery, and burglary.[38]

aggression, but at least in this experiment it could not be factored out as the cause of aggression.

Alcohol has been referred to as a social lubricant. That is, after an individual consumes alcohol, he or she will talk more, more loudly, and aggressively. This response was thought to be suggestive and proceeded to aggression. To control for the suggestive effect, large doses of alcohol were administered intravenously.[27] The individuals were then placed in a social situation, unaware that they were receiving alcohol. These individuals exhibited aggressive and boisterous behavior and thus, at least in this study, it was the alcohol and not the suggestive effect that released the negative behavior.

Aggression and its relationship to alcohol may be culturally determined. Men have been led to believe that alcohol leads to aggression in men[28] and sexual behavior in women. Women have been led to believe that alcohol leads to sexual behavior in men and women. An explanation may be that women most frequently drink in mixed company while men drink mainly with other men.

☐ Theories and evidence

Alcohol is postulated to affect aggressive-related behaviors through biochemical action. Studies have indicated that an individual's level of epinephrine secretion is significantly higher after drinking than before drinking. Continuing research is attempting to determine the relationship of biomedical action to observed changes in behavior.[29]

Drinking behavior has been related to needs for power that accompany drinking. Individuals who had higher power needs were more likely to drink heavily than those with lower power needs. Aggressive fantasies and sexual imagery were found to be increased during drinking. The illusion of power during drinking creates positive feedback and thus promotes continued drinking.

Another view is that alcohol uninhibits and thus facilitates aggression by. reducing fear of the social consequences of aggression. Alcohol seemed to provide the stimulus for the individual to exhibit repressed aggressive activity. Individuals talk more and louder when drinking moderately. Heavy drinking has been correlated with verbal aggression, violent arguments, and assault.[29,30]

A recent explanation regarding the effects of alcohol on aggressive behavior[31] is the expectancy factor. Male social drinkers were randomly assigned to study groups. To control for expectation effects, half of the sample were led to believe that they would be drinking alcohol and half believed they would be drinking only tonic. Within each of these groups, half of the men actually received alcohol and half received only tonic. This design isolated the effects of expectation.

The most important finding was that differences in the level of aggression could be explained by the expectation of the beverage they consumed. The men who believed they were drinking alcohol were more aggressive than those who believed they were drinking only tonic regardless of alcoholic content. This study suggests that the expectancy factor may explain the correlation between alcohol and aggression.

Alcohol may provide a convenient excuse for individuals who want to behave in an aggressive manner . . . verbally or physically. The drinker may then avoid the responsibility for the aggressive behavior by attributing it to the effects of alcohol. Alcohol facilitates aggression by an expectancy factor, a cue, or uninhibitor. The aggression may be heightened by some biochemical action. The evidence is incontrovertible, however, that alcohol and aggression are correlated.

■ SUMMARY

After analyzing the theories and evidence related to alcohol and aggression, there appears to be a strong but unexplainable correlation between the consumption of alcohol and aggressive behavior. The physiological evidence is not conclusive regarding the biochemical and etiological association of alcohol to aggression. Also, some studies produce conflicting results because of the difficulty of controlling variables, especially in direct observation studies. There is, however, ample behavioral evidence in the areas of criminal activity, student problems, and automobile accidents to justify the theoretical relationship between alcohol and aggression. The bottom line is simple. Heavy drinkers engage in more aggressive activity than moderate or light drinkers.

REFERENCES

1. National Institute of Law Enforcement and Criminal Justice, Law Enforcement Assistance Administration: Alcohol and crime: reference services statistics, Washington, D.C., 1976, U.S. Department of Justice.
2. Brecher, E. M.: Licit and illicit drugs, Boston, 1972, Little, Brown and Co., p. 262.
3. Dennison, D.: The effects of selected field experiences upon the drinking behavior of university students, J. Sch. Health **44:**16-24, 1974.
4. Barton, W. E.: Deficits in treatment of alcoholism and recommendations for correction, Am. J. Psychiatr. **124:**1679-1686, 1968.
5. King, L. J., Murphy, G. E., Robins, L. N., and Darvish, H.: Alcohol abuse: a crucial factor in the social problems of Negro men, Am. J. Psychiatr. **125:**1682-1690, 1969.
6. Goodwin, D. W.: Alcohol in suicide and homicide, J. Stud. Alcohol **34:**144-156, 1973.

7. Haberman, P. W., and Baden, M. D.: Alcoholism and violent death, J. Stud. Alcohol **35:**221-231, 1974.
8. Mayfield, D.: Alcoholism, alcohol, intoxication and assaultive behavior, Dis. Nerv. Syst. **37:**288-291, 1976.
9. Pearce, J., and Garrett, H. D.: A comparison of the drinking behavior of delinquent youth versus non-delinquent youth in the states of Idaho and Utah, J. Sch. Health **40:**131-135, 1970.
10. Globetti, G.: The use of beverage alcohol by youth in and abstinence setting, J. Sch. Health **39:**179-183, 1969.
11. Kane, R. L., and Patterson, E.: Drinking attitudes and behaviors of high school students in Kentucky, J. Stud. Alcohol **33:**635-646, 1972.
12. Wechsler, H., and Thum, D.: Teenage drinking, drug use, and social correlates, J. Stud. Alcohol **34:**1220-1227, 1973.
13. Barnes, G. M.: A perspective on drinking among teenagers with special reference to New York State studies, J. Sch. Health **45:**386-389, 1975.
14. Mandell, W., et al.: Youthful drinking—New York State, 1962, Staten Island, N.Y., 1962, Staten Island Mental Health Society.
15. LeMay, M.: College disciplinary referrals for drinking, J. Stud. Alcohol **29:**939-942, 1968.
16. Waller, J.: Factors associated with alcohol and responsibility for fatal highway crashes, J. Stud. Alcohol **33:**160-170, 1972.
17. Campbell, H.: The roll of alcohol in fatal traffic accidents and measures needed to solve the problem, Mich. Med. **63:**699-703, 1964.
18. Waller, J., et al.: Alcohol and other factors in California highway fatalities, J. Forensic Sci. **14:**429-443, 1969.
19. McCarrol, J., and Haddon, W.: A controlled study of fatal automobile accidents in New York City, J. Chron. Dis. **15:**811-826, 1961.
20. Pelz, D., McDole, T. L., and Schuman, S. H.: Drinking-driving behavior of young men in relation to accidents, J. Stud. Alcohol **36:**956-972, 1975.
21. Rosenberg, N., Laessig, R. H., and Rawlings, R. R.: Alcohol, age and fatal traffic accidents, J. Stud. Alcohol **35:**473-489, 1974.
22. Zylman, R.: Accidents, alcohol and single-cause explanations, J. Stud. Alcohol **29**(suppl. 4):212-233, 1968.
23. Smart, R. G., and Wolfgang, S.: Blood alcohol levels in drivers not involved in accidents, J. Stud. Alcohol **31:**968-971, 1970.
24. Selzer, M. L., and Weiss, S.: Alcoholism and traffic fatalities: study in futility, Am. J. Psychiatr. **122:**762-767, 1965.
25. Bennet, R. M., Buss, A. H., and Carpenter, J. A.: Alcohol and human physical aggression, J. Stud. Alcohol **30:**870-876, 1969.
26. Buss, A. H., Carpenter, J. A., Bennet, R. M., and Buss, E. H.: Alcohol and aggression in women, 1969, Unpublished.
27. Hartocollis, P.: Drunkenness and suggestion: an experiment with intravenous alcohol, J. Stud. Alcohol **23:**376-389, 1962.
28. Carpenter, J. A., and Armenti, N. P.: Some effects of ethanol on human sexual and aggressive behavior, In Kissin, B., and Begleiter, H.: The biology of alcoholism. II. Physiology and behavior, New York, 1972, Plenum Press, pp. 509-543.
29. Dotson, L. E., Robertson, L. S., and Tuchfeld, B.: Plasma alcohol, smoking, hormone concentrations and self-reported aggression: a study in a social-drinking situation, J. Stud. Alcohol **30**(5):578-586, 1975.
30. Boyatzis, R. E.: The effect of alcohol consumption on the aggressive behavior of men, J. Stud. Alcohol **35:**959-972, 1974.

31. Lang, A., Goeckner, D., Adesso, V., and Marlatt, G.; Effects of alcohol on aggression in male social drinkers, J. Abnorm. Psychol. **84**(5):508-518, 1975.
32. Boyatzis, R.: The predisposition toward alcohol-related interpersonal aggression in men, J. Stud. Alcohol **36**:1196-1207, 1975.
33. Warren, G. H., and Raynes, A. E.: Mood changes during three conditions of alcohol intake, J. Stud. Alcohol **22**:979-989, 1972.
34. Hartocollis, P.: Drunkenness and suggestion: an experiment with intravenous alcohol, J. Stud. Alcohol **23**:376-389, 1962.
35. Hetherington, E. M., and Wray, N. P.: Aggression, need for social approval and humor preference, J. Pers. Soc. Psychol. **68**:685-689, 1964.
36. Kalin, R., McClelland, D. C., and Kahn, M.: The effects of male social drinking on fantasy, J. Pers. Soc. Psychol. **1**:441-452, 1965.
37. Shupe, L. M.: Alcohol and crime: a study of the urine alcohol concentration found in 882 persons arrested during or immediately after the commission of a felony, J. Crim. Law Criminals **44**:661-664, 1954.
38. Wolfgand, M., and Strohm, R. B.: The relationship between alcohol and criminal homicide, J. Stud. Alcohol **17**:411-425, 1956.

Part II

COGNITIVE PHASE

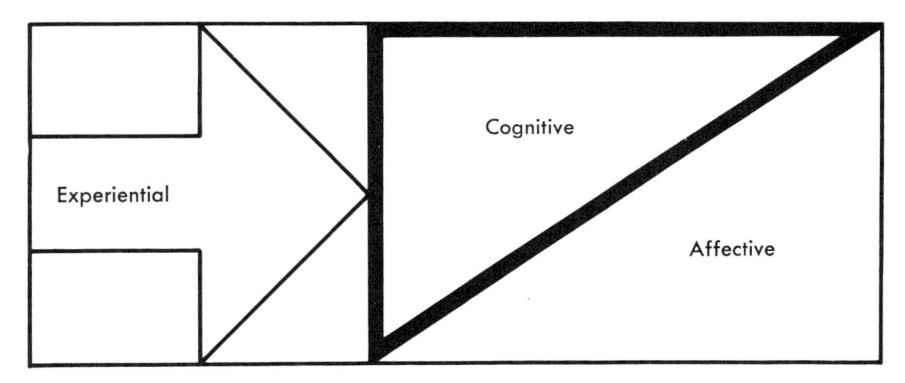

Schema for activated health education.

4 THE DISEASE PROCESS

The disease concept of alcoholism as it relates to both physiological and psychosocial health is presented in this chapter. The consumer is made aware of the long-term physical and psychological consequences of alcohol abuse. The ramifications of the repetitive use of alcohol and the degenerative process of the disease alcoholism are explained. After reading the chapter and noting the specific characteristic changes in health that take place as a result of alcohol use, an individual is more apt to feel personally susceptible to alcohol-related problems.

Health is a difficult concept to define. The health status of an individual can be best described by using a continuum concept. An individual's health can be measured in degrees or stages and can be placed somewhere along this health status continuum. This continuum, with its various gradations, extends from optimal health at one end of the scale to critical illness at the other.

Four levels of physiological and psychosocial health can be used to describe the health status of the individual on the continuum. The four levels consist of optimal health, incipient illness, overt illness, and critical illness. Specific physiological and psychosocial characteristics can be identified at various stages.

■ HEALTH STATUS CONTINUUM
□ Optimal health

When individuals are classified as being optimally healthy, they fall somewhere on a continuum between being able to perform the minimal daily functions of life to being able to function in highly strenuous activity. Persons' physiological health depends a great deal on their needs and lifestyle. Although a sedentary person and a professional athlete may both be classified as being in optimal health physiologically, the professional athlete is more likely to possess greater physiological efficiency and therefore have a higher degree of optimal health than the sedentary individual. In our society very few individuals ever reach extremely high levels of optimal physiological health and they seldom maintain it over an extended period of time. Most individuals are found at the middle or lower end of the continuum.

Individuals in optimal health from a psychosocial standpoint possess a positive self-image and feel good about themselves. They usually have quality interpersonal relationships and a wide range of friends. They have learned to live with themselves and to cope effectively with their environment. Persons feeling this way and engaging in these activities are enjoying optimal health.

Incipient illness

In this stage of the health continuum the individual's health begins to deteriorate and physiological problems become evident. During this period the onset of nonspecific illness symptoms occurs. The individual may suffer from such discomforts as headache, nausea, mild fever, nasal discharge, and sore throat. Specific diagnosis as to whether the individual is suffering from a common cold or a more serious illness is difficult to determine at this time. These physiological discomforts may lead the individual to stop engaging in all nonessential activities.

In the psychosocial realm the individual's behavior may be described as variant. The individual begins to have difficulty in relating to others and is easily upset by the usual daily annoyances. As illness progresses, there is dissatisfaction with oneself and others, and because of repetitive problems with others, the individual begins to isolate from society.

Table 4. Health status continuum

Physiological characteristics	Psychosocial characteristics
Optimal health	
Wide range of physiological efficiency	Behavior described as normal
Highly active to sedentary individual	Individual copes effectively with environment
Ability to perform highly strenuous activity to being able to perform just minimal daily activity	Feels good about self
	Quality interpersonal relationships
	Wide range of friends
Depends on needs and lifestyle	Positive self-image
Incipient illness	
Deteriorating health	Behavior described as variant
Individual experiences physiological problems	Difficulty in relating to others
	Easily upset
Nonspecific illness symptoms appear	Repetitive problems
	Begins isolating self
Difficult diagnosis	
Nonessential activities cease	
Overt illness	
Disease diagnosed	Behavior described as deviant
Minimal activity level	Extremely anxious individuals
Use of drugs	Therapy recommended
Hospitalization may be necessary	Institutionalization may be necessary
Critical illness	
Very poor health	Psychotic
Vital signs unstable	Loss of touch with reality
Hospitalization necessary	Cannot cope with environment
	Psychiatric help and hospitalization necessary

☐ Overt illness

In the overt illness stage of the health continuum specific disease symptoms appear and the individual may be clinically diagnosed as having a particular disease. Usually the activity level of the individual is kept to a minimum, and in some cases isolation is necessary to prevent the spread of the disease. In order to alter the normal course of the disease, chemotherapy is often used. Confinement including hospitalization is sometimes necessary.

Psychosocially, individuals in this stage of illness are extremely anxious. Behaviors of these individuals are deviant and tend to interfere with normal functioning. Establishing close relationships with others becomes difficult, and these individuals no longer engage in social interaction with any positive aspects. Persons are sometimes described as neurotic, and therapy is required for rehabilitation. Institutionalization is sometimes recommended.

☐ Critical illness

In the critical illness stage of the health continuum the physical health of the individual is very poor. Vital life signs are unstable and hospitalization is often necessary.

Individuals experiencing critical psychosocial illness are classified as psychotic. They have deteriorated to a point where there is personality disintegration and loss of contact with reality. They have difficulty making correct interpretations about themselves and their environment. They are unable to cope with the world around them, and they have little control over what they do. They cannot care for themselves, and psychiatric help and hospitalization are necessary (Table 4).

THE SPIDER-WEB

Whenever I see
On bush or tree
A great big spider-web
I say with a shout,
"Little fly, look out!
That web seems so pretty and white,
But a spider hides there, and is ready to bite."
So if any one here
Drinks cider or beer
I say to him now,
With my very best bow,
"Have a care of that lager or cider,
For there hides a wicked old spider,
And it fills him with joy
To catch man or boy
And weave all about him with terrible might
The meshes of habit-the rum appetite."

Selected from *The Late Demon Rum**
J. C. FURNAS

---

*International Temperance Association, 6840 Eastern Ave., N. W., Washington, D.C.

ALCOHOL ABUSE AND THE HEALTH CONTINUUM

Problems associated with the use of alcohol are cumulative. These problems follow the health status continuum from social drinking in the optimal health category to severe psychosis caused by alcoholism in the critical illness stage.

Alcoholism is a disease with the etiology being mainly psychosocial and the ramifications both physiological and psychosocial. Alcohol is a necessary ingredient in the development of problem drinking; however, it is not the only one. A vast majority of social drinkers never become problem drinkers. Only a small percentage of alcohol problems are believed to have a physiological origin with theories relating to endocrine malfunction, metabolic disturbances, and biochemical imbalances being cited as causes. The majority of alcohol-related problems are believed to be psychosocial in nature. Alcohol seems to have maximum appeal to individuals who have difficulty dealing with stress, depression, anxiety and frustration.

The following discussion describes both the physiological and psychosocial characteristics of alcohol use as it relates to the stages of health.

Optimal health

Social drinkers and nondrinkers are considered optimally healthy. Social drinking does not physiologically harm individuals. The actual amounts of alcohol ingested without being harmful vary among individuals. Most individuals can drink approximately one to two drinks, resulting in a blood alcohol level of 0.053 without marked impairment.

Social drinking does no harm psychologically. The amounts of alcohol that would be harmful vary greatly with the person and his or her environment.

MYTH: YOU REALLY HAVE TO ADMIRE PEOPLE WHO CAN HOLD THEIR LIQUOR.

One should not be envious of people who are capable of holding their liquor. If a person possesses the ability to drink large quantities of alcohol without feeling the normal effects, it means that this individual has probably developed a tolerance to alcohol. A tolerance develops from chronic use of alcohol. It results from the body adaptation to the continual presence of alcohol. Once tolerance develops, the person is not affected by the amounts of alcohol that normally affect other people. The individual requires continually larger amounts to produce the desired effects. This adaptation process is believed to be the result of changes in all metabolism. Tolerance usually indicates the onset of dependency and addiction.

When a person becomes dependent on alcohol, the body needs it both physiologically and psychologically in order to function. Dependency results from the adaptation of the cells in the brain to the presence of alcohol. When dependency occurs, if alcohol is taken away, the user experiences withdrawal symptoms. These withdrawal symptoms are severe physiological discomforts characterized by stomach cramps, nausea, shakes, delirium, and sometimes hallucinations.

Therefore why should we admire tolerance? It just means that the person is just one step closer to becoming one of the 9.5 million drinkers in the United States dependent on alcohol.

☐ Incipient illness

At the incipient illness level, physiological harm to individuals can be temporary or permanent. When physiological harm occurs on a temporary basis, the blood alcohol level of individuals may reach a level of 0.05 to 0.08. At this blood alcohol level visual and hearing activity is reduced and slight speech impairment and minor disturbance of balance occur. Increased difficulty in performing motor skills and slowed reaction time are also observed. Once the alcohol has been oxidized by the body and functioning returns to normal, individuals are once again considered in optimal health. Permanent physiological harm occurs when alcohol is used repetitively over lengthy periods of time.

Psychosocially, individuals move along the continuum from an occasional problem drinker to a repetitive problem drinker. Continual and excessive drinking causes physical, psychological, and social harm to the individual and others.

At the lower level of incipient illness, patterns of drinking lead to frequent intoxication and other socially unacceptable behavior. The drinking disturbs interpersonal relationships. At this phase drinkers associate mainly with people who exhibit the same type of alcohol-related behaviors. Drinking begins to affect employment status and relationships with family and friends.

☐ Overt illness

In the overt illness stage, individuals develop an increased tolerance to alcohol and are dependent on it. As the body adapts to the repetitive use of alcohol, individuals need continually greater amounts of alcohol to achieve the desired effects. Alcohol is necessary for these individuals to function. If deprived of alcohol, they experience withdrawal symptoms characterized by mild confusion, muscle tremors, delirium, and sometimes hallucinations. Individuals in this phase are now compulsive drinkers who have lost control over rates and amounts of their alcohol consumption. These individuals are preoccupied with alcohol and consistently drink to the point of intoxication. Cirrhosis of the liver, gastritis, nutritional problems, and other physical disabilities related to alcohol abuse may exist at this time.

Psychological as well as a physiological dependence on alcohol is present at this stage of the illness. The disease is classified as alcoholism and the social, psychological, and responsibility levels of the individuals have decreased. These individuals are often arrested for drunkenness, driving while intoxicated, or other alcohol-related problems. Their antisocial behavior may result in loss of job, alienation of friends, disruption of family, or separation of family. During this stage the alcoholic tends to drink alone or with other alcoholics or heavy drinkers. Under pressure from family or employer, alcoholics may attempt to quit drinking or to seek medical help. Chances of rehabilitation at this time may be described as poor.

☐ Critical illness

At the critical illness stage, physiological deterioration has reached a point where tissues and organs have been seriously affected. Liver damage may be severe. Damage

36 COGNITIVE PHASE

Table 5. Alcohol abuse and the health continuum

Physiological characteristics	Psychological characteristics
Optimal health	
Social drinkers	Social drinking has no
Harmful effects vary with	psychological harm
individuals and environment	Harmful amounts vary with
Usually one to two drinks	individual and environment
without marked impairment	
Incipient illness	
Physiological harm can be	Ranges from occasional problem
temporary or permanent	drinking to repetitive problem
Temporary—when BAC is at	drinking
0.05 or greater	Frequent intoxication
Permanent harm—through	Socially unacceptable behavior
repetitive use of alcohol	Associates with alcoholic and
	heavy drinkers
	Drinking affects relationships
Overt illness	
Increased tolerance	Disease classified as alcoholism
Alcohol dependency	Alcohol-related problems exist
Loss of control—consistently	Antisocial behavior prevalent
drinks to intoxication	Drinks alone or with other
Physical problems may exist	alcoholics
	Chances of rehabilitation
	described as poor
Critical illness	
Physical deterioration exists	Severe psychological problems
Damage to liver, stomach,	Psychiatric help and
and nervous system	hospitalization necessary
Experiences severe withdrawal	Chances of rehabilitation are slim
when deprived	

to the nervous system may result in delirium tremens (DTs). Delirium tremens is characterized by uncontrollable shaking, convulsions, and visual hallucinations. Wernicke syndrome is another condition that results from the dietary deficiencies associated with alcohol abuse. This condition affects the brain and results in loss of mental acuity, paralysis of eye muscles, and disturbances in balance and coordination. If brain damage becomes severe, alcoholics may require care for the remainder of their lives.

When alcoholics reach this final stage, they usually have severe psychological impairment. They have unexplainable fears, a sense of impending doom, and need alcohol as their psychological crutch. At this time, psychiatric help and hospitalization are necessary, and the probability of rehabilitation is slim (Table 5).

■ SUMMARY

Information is presented to the consumer concerning the relationship of alcohol-related behavior and general health. A continuum with stages of health ranging from optimal health to critical illness is used. Various physiological and psychosocial characteristics of health are identifiable at each of these stages.

In terms of physiological health, optimally healthy individuals possess a degree of health that enables them to participate in at least a minimum of daily activities. When an individual enters the incipient illness stage, the onset and discomfort of the nonspecific illness usually brings activity levels of the individual to a minimum. In the overt illness stage, diagnosis of the illness is now possible. Medication and bedrest or hospitalization are usually prescribed. If the disease progresses to the critical illness stage, chances of survival for the individual are usually precarious.

Psychosocially, the individual can also progress through the full range of the health continuum. Normal individuals, because of many types of circumstances, can find themselves becoming dissatisfied with themselves and others. Abnormal behavior and isolation can result. Behaviors can become more extreme and interfere with normal functioning. Illness can progress to a point where behaviors are described as psychotic and hospitalization and psychiatric help are necessary.

The consumer is also presented with the relationship between alcohol-related behavior and the health continuum. The consumer is made cognizant of the signs and symptoms of alcoholism at various stages on the health continuum. Both the physiological and psychosocial aspects of alcohol use and abuse are discussed. Hopefully, an awareness of the ramifications of excessive drinking will minimize the personal risk of tragic alcoholism for the consumer.

SOMETHING TO YOU

" 'Tis nothing to me," the beauty said,
With a careless toss of her pretty head;
"The man is weak if he can't refrain
From the cup you say is fraught with pain."

It was something when, in after-years,
Her eyes were drenched with burning tears,
And she watched in lonely grief and dread,
And startled to hear a staggering tread.

" 'Tis nothing to me." the mother said:
"I have no fear that my boy will tread
In the downward path of sin and shame
And crush my heart and darken his name."

It was something to her when her only son
From the path of right was early won,
And madly cast in the flowing bowl
A ruined body, a sin-wrecked soul.

" 'Tis nothing to me," the merchant said,
As over his ledger he bent his head;
"I am busy to-day with tare and tret,
I have no time for fume and fret."

It was something to him when over the wire
A message came for a funeral pyre;
A drunken conductor had wrecked a train,
And his wife and child were among the slain.

" 'Tis nothing to me," the voter said;
'The party's loss is my only dread.''
Then he gave his vote to the liquor trade,
Though hearts were crushed and drunkards made.

It was something to him in after-life;
His daughter became a drunkard's wife,
And her hungry children cried for bread,
And trembled to hear their father's tread.

It is something for us to idly sleep,
While cohorts of death their vigils keep,
To gather the young and thoughtless in,
And grind in our midst a grist of sin.

Selected from *The Late Demon Rum**
J. C. FURNAS

*International Temperance Association, 6840 Eastern Ave., N.W., Washington, D.C.

5 BIOLOGICAL DIMENSION

In this chapter, information is presented concerning the pharmacological properties of alcohol and the effects of alcohol on the body. The factors associated with the absorption of alcohol in the body, the physiological effects of alcohol at various blood alcohol levels, and the process by which alcohol is removed from the body are explained. Information surrounding the use of alcohol and the long-term effects of alcohol on the stomach, liver, endocrine system, and the heart are reviewed. The chapter offers the consumer the relevant information and terminology necessary for understanding the empirical research presented in the next chapter. The information will also aid in making intelligent decisions concerning the use of alcohol.

Alcohol is a chemical compound made up of carbon, hydrogen, and oxygen. Many different types of alcohol can be produced by varying the proportions of each of these three elements. One of these alcohols is ethanol, the intoxicating fluid found in all alcoholic beverages.

■ PROPERTIES

Ethanol, or ethyl alcohol, is composed of two carbon atoms, five hydrogen atoms, and one hydroxyl group (composed of one oxygen atom and one hydrogen atom).

$$C_2 - H_5 - OH$$

When this clear, colorless liquid with a pungent taste and very little odor is taken internally, it has a toxic effect on the body. A slight irritation to the lining of the mouth, esophagus, and stomach results when alcohol is consumed. Even though alco-

---

MYTH: ALCOHOL CAN BE USED AS A FOOD SUPPLEMENT.

Alcohol has no nutritional value and is not classified as a food. No vitamins, minerals, or proteins are contained in alcohol. Alcohol's chief value is in the calories it provides for the body.

A significant amount of calories is contained in alcohol. Since alcohol is not stored in the body, it is metabolized to produce a source of immediate energy equivalent to seven calories per gram of alcohol. This immediate energy source allows food normally used in energy production to be converted into fat and stored in the body. When eating habits of a heavy drinker remain unchanged as alcohol intake increases, weight gains can result. However, alcohol usually depresses the appetite of the heavy drinker and causes dietary problems. This leads to nutritional deficiencies, which causes liver and neurological disorders in heavy drinkers and alcoholics.

hol is considered toxic, ethyl alcohol is the only alcohol that can be safely consumed. Consumption of any other type can be extremely dangerous.

Ethyl alcohol is capable of being mixed with water and diffusing through body membranes. Once absorbed into the body, it acts as a depressant on the central nervous system. Alcohol is not stored in the body but metabolized immediately to provide an immediate source of energy.

■ ALCOHOLIC BEVERAGES

The ethyl alcohol contained in all alcoholic beverages is formed through a natural fermentation process. This process converts sugars, naturally occurring in plants, into alcohol and carbon dioxide with yeast cells acting as the catalyst.

$$C_2H_{12}O_6 \xrightarrow{Yeast} 2C_2H_5OH + 2CO_2$$
$$\text{Sugar} \qquad\qquad \text{Alcohol} \quad \text{Carbon dioxide}$$

The fermentation process takes place until the sugar content of the grain or fruit juice is used or until the yeast dies due to high concentrations of alcohol being produced. Yeast cells have a low tolerance to alcohol and usually die when the concentration of alcohol reaches between 12% and 14% of the total volume.

In producing wine, it is usually the juice of the grape that is allowed to ferment. Since natural fermentation ceases when alcohol concentrations reach 14%, most wine contains around that amount of alcohol. Some wines such as sherry and vermouth have plain alcohol or brandy added to them. These fortified wines contain as much as 24% alcohol.

Like wine, beer is made from a fermentation process; however, grain is the chief ingredient rather than fruit or grape juice. During this process the starch in the grain is converted to sugar by malt enzymes and then allowed to ferment. Beer contains around 4% alcohol by volume, while malt liquor and ale have somewhat higher concentrations.

MYTH: ALCOHOL WARMS THE BODY.

The vasoconstrictor center in the brain is affected by the depressant action of alcohol. When this center, located in the medulla, is depressed by the action of alcohol, the small blood vessels in the skin become dilated. The dilation of these normally constricted blood vessels causes increased blood flow to the skin. This results in a flushing of the skin and a feeling of warmth for the drinker. This warming sensation leads drinkers to believe that alcoholic beverages warm the body. As a result, people will drink alcohol to warm themselves. Unfortunately for the individual who drinks for this reason, the action of alcohol will actually have a reverse effect.

When alcohol is consumed, heat is lost rapidly through the skin. Normally, on a cold day, blood vessels in the skin are constricted to conserve heat loss. As a result of the action of alcohol, heat is lost when the peripheral blood vessels in the skin dilate. This heat loss causes a lowering of internal body temperature. Therefore, as one consumes alcohol, heat loss is enhanced and the person becomes colder.

When fermented beverages are carried a step further through a process known as distillation, beverages with higher alcohol concentration may be produced. Distillation is a process by which substances are separated by an evaporation-condensation technique. Since alcohol has a lower boiling point (173 F or 78.3 C) than the other substances found in fermented mixtures, it can be boiled off and collected at higher alcohol concentrations. This distillate, which is collected after it passes through a series of coil pipes, averages about 45% alcohol by volume. The alcohol concentration of these distillates or distilled spirits is indicated by the term "proof" on the bottle. The percentage of alcohol in the distilled spirits is always one half the proof number. Therefore ninety proof wiskey would contain 45% alcohol volume. The term proof originated with the British military. In order to gauge the alcohol content of the distilled spirits to be purchased, small amounts of the liquid would be mixed with gunpowder and lit. If the mixture ignited, it was "proof" that the distilled spirits contained at least 50% alcohol. Weaker alcohol concentrations existed if the mixture failed to ignite.

ALCOHOL ABSORPTION

Alcohol is a chemically simple substance that requires no chemical breakdown when it is ingested into the body. When alcohol enters the stomach, it diffuses through the walls of the stomach and is absorbed immediately into the bloodstream. Within a few minutes after ingestion, alcohol is detectable in the blood. Peak alcohol concentrations are reached within an hour. Approximately 20% of the alcohol ingested is absorbed in the stomach, while the remaining 80% is absorbed primarily in the duodenal area of the small intestine (Fig. 7). The rate at which alcohol diffuses through the walls of the digestive tract is influenced by the following factors:

1. *Alcohol concentration.* As a general rule, the greater the concentration of alcohol in the beverage, the more rapidly the alcohol is absorbed into the bloodstream. The rate of absorption is most rapid when the alcohol concentrations are below 40% (80 proof). When the concentration of alcohol exceeds this level, the rate of absorption tends to be slower.
2. *Rate of consumption.* The speed at which alcohol is consumed affects the rate of absorption. If an individual "downs" or "chugs" one or several drinks rapidly, a higher blood alcohol level will result than if one drinks more slowly.
3. *Amount of alcohol.* The time necessary for complete absorption of alcohol depends on the amount of alcohol ingested. The greater the quantity of alcohol consumed, the more time required for total absorption.
4. *Chemicals present in the alcoholic beverage.* The nonalcoholic chemicals present in an alcoholic beverage slow the absorption process. Beer and wine have a slower absorption rate than distilled spirits because they contain a greater amount of nonalcoholic chemicals. These substances tend to dilute and lower the alcohol concentration of the beverage.

If alcoholic beverages are mixed with other substances, such as orange juice or water, the absorption of alcohol is delayed. However, if alcohol is mixed

42 COGNITIVE PHASE

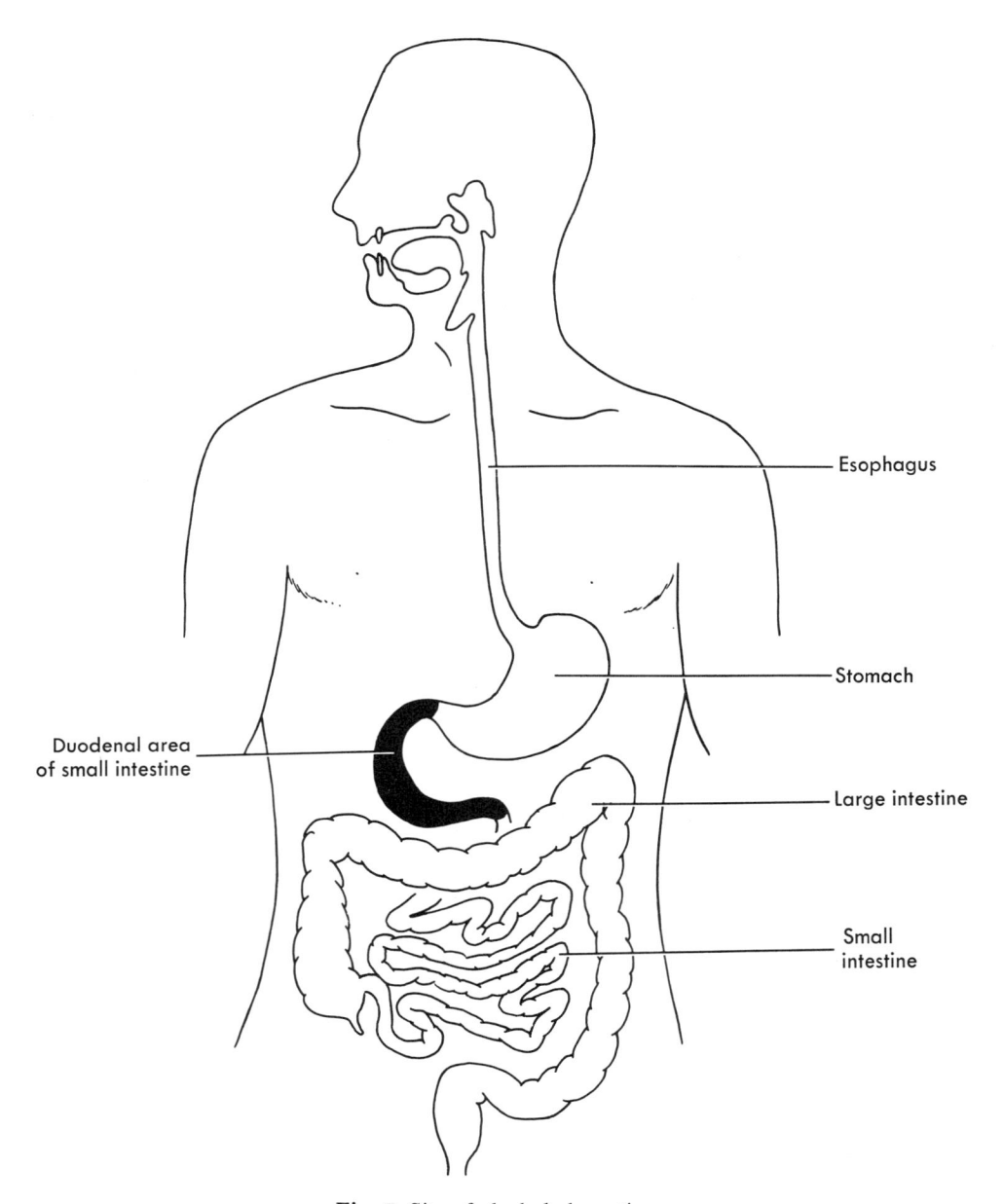

Fig. 7. Site of alcohol absorption.

with a carbonated beverage, the absorption rate is sped up. When carbon dioxide is present in the stomach, the pylorus, a sphincter muscle that holds foodstuff in the stomach, relaxes and permits the alcohol to pass from the stomach into the small intestine where it is absorbed more readily.

5. *Condition of the stomach.* The presence of food in the stomach slows the absorption rate of alcohol. When alcohol mixes with food in the stomach, it re-

mains there until the digestive process is complete. Foods such as protein and fat have a complex chemical makeup and remain in the stomach for a considerable length of time, while carbohydrates remain for shorter periods of time. With alcohol remaining in the stomach for the complete digestion of all foods, the rate of absorption is reduced considerably. Maximum blood alcohol levels can be reduced significantly by eating before or during drinking.

6. *Pylorospasm.* When alcohol enters the digestive tract, it causes irritation to the lining of the stomach. In some cases the pyloric valve, a ring of muscle at the lower end of the stomach, becomes irritated and closes tightly. This spasm or involuntary contraction of the muscle prevents the alcohol from leaving the stomach and entering the upper portion of the small intestines. With alcohol remaining in the stomach, absorption is slowed. If the irritation from the alcohol persists, nausea and vomiting can result.

7. *Emotional condition.* Emotional states such as fear, anxiety, and anger can affect the absorption rate of alcohol. The mood of an individual affects the involuntary nervous system and can affect the pyloric valve. The pyloric valve, in turn, controls the speed at which alcohol leaves the stomach and is absorbed in the small intestines. When a person is under stress and tension, alcohol seems to be absorbed faster and has a faster effect than when a person drinks in a relaxed, comfortable setting.

■ DISTRIBUTION

After alcohol diffuses through the walls of the stomach and small intestine, it is carried to all parts of the body via the bloodstream. Most drugs travel through the blood attached to protein molecules; however, alcohol has a low affinity for becoming protein bound and travels primarily in the blood in an unbound state. Alcohol's physiological effects begin to occur almost immediately as a result of being distributed in an unbound state. Those drugs that travel protein bound have a slow onset of effects. The duration of effect, however, is shorter for alcohol than for the protein-bound drugs.[1]

■ BLOOD ALCOHOL CONCENTRATION

The concentration of alcohol in any one tissue or organ depends on the fluid content on that tissue or organ. The blood with a high water content is a tissue where high concentrations of alcohol are found. By measuring the BAC, the amount of alcohol that has been absorbed into the body can be determined. The BAC, which is expressed in a percentage, is the ratio of alcohol present in the blood in comparison to the total blood volume.

Body size is a factor in determining BAC. A large individual has more body fluid to dilute the alcohol than a small individual. If they both consumed the same amount of alcohol, the larger person would have a lower BAC level. Therefore a large person can consume greater quantities of alcohol than a small one and experience fewer effects. Table 6 presents the blood alcohol concentration in relation to body weight and the amount of drinks consumed.

Table 6. Relationship of body weight to driving ability by blood alcohol concentrations (%)*

Body weight (lb)	Number of alcoholic beverages†												
	1	2	3	4	5	6	7	8	9	10	11	12
100	0.038	0.075	0.113	0.150	0.188	0.225	0.263	0.300	0.338	0.375	0.413	0.450
120	0.031	0.063	0.094	0.125	0.156	0.188	0.219	0.250	0.281	0.313	0.344	0.375
140	0.027	0.054	0.080	0.107	0.134	0.161	0.188	0.214	0.241	0.268	0.295	0.321
160	0.023	0.047	0.070	0.094	0.117	0.141	0.164	0.188	0.211	0.234	0.258	0.281
180	0.021	0.042	0.063	0.083	0.104	0.125	0.146	0.167	0.188	0.208	0.229	0.250
200	0.019	0.038	0.056	0.075	0.094	0.113	0.131	0.150	0.169	0.188	0.206	0.225
220	0.017	0.034	0.051	0.068	0.085	0.102	0.119	0.136	0.153	0.170	0.188	0.205
240	0.016	0.031	0.047	0.063	0.078	0.094	0.109	0.125	0.141	0.156	0.172	0.188
	Under 0.05: driving is not seriously impaired			0.05 to 0.10: driving becomes increasingly dangerous; 0.08 legally drunk in Utah			0.10 to 0.15: driving is dangerous; legally drunk in most states			Over 0.15: driving is very dangerous; legally drunk in any state		

*Reprinted through the courtesy of the New Jersey Department of Law and Public Safety, Division of Motor Vehicles, Trenton, N.J.
†One drink equals one ounce of 100 proof liquor or 12 ounces of beer.

Another factor in determining BAC is the sex of the individual. Me body fluids then women of the same weight. Therefore the concentration o be lower in the man than in the woman when the same amounts of alcohol are sumed.

■ EFFECTS OF ALCOHOL

Alcohol is a depressant drug that slows certain body functions by depressing the entire central nervous system. Researchers believe that alcohol acts on the central nervous system by interfering with the nerve cells' ability to produce electrical impulses and transmit them across the synapse. This depressant effect of alcohol on the central nervous system is directly related to the BAC. As BAC increases and the action of alcohol depresses the brain and nervous system, the behavior of the drinker is altered. Table 7 reports the general behavioral characteristics that are present at the various BACs. In general, at very low BACs a drinker tends to feel euphoric and relaxed. As BAC increases, the drinker may become aggressive, confused, depressed, and drowsy. At very high levels unconsciousness, coma, and death can result.

The effects of alcohol are noticeable even after the first drink. At a 0.01 to 0.03 BAC the drinker experiences a sense of warmth, a mild tranquilizing effect, and a feeling of general well-being. As the BAC increases, the drinker experiences a greater feeling of relaxation and encounters difficulty in performing fine motor skills. Researchers have found that at very low BAC (0.02 to 0.05), stability of stance, reaction time, psychomotor performance, and mental performance are affected. At approximately the 0.08 BAC level, visual and hearing acuity is reduced, coordination is impaired, and inhibitions and restraints tend to disappear. In some states a person driving an automobile with a BAC of 0.07 to 0.09 would be considered driving while impaired. If convicted, the person could have his or her driver's license suspended for 60 days.

MYTH: ALCOHOL IS A STIMULANT DRUG.

Alcohol is often thought of as being a stimulant drug; however, because of the sedative effect it has on the brain and central nervous system, alcohol is classified as a depressant. The depressant effect of alcohol occurs even when only small quantities of alcohol are consumed. One of the first areas of the brain to be affected by alcohol is the cerebral cortex, the center of judgment, self-control, and inhibitions. The depression of this portion of the brain often results in excitable forms of behavior in people due to a loss of inhibitions and social restraints. This type of reaction to the depressant effect of alcohol often leads people to believe alcohol is a stimulant drug.

When large quantities of alcohol are consumed, the depressant effects become even greater. After depression of the cerebral cortex, the effects of alcohol progress to the lower brain centers. Eventually at very high blood alcohol levels, the medulla is affected. The medulla is responsible for the control of vital functions. This area of the brain can become so dangerously depressed that both respiratory and cardiac functioning may cease. This most severe form of alcohol depression is not uncommon and often occurs in unsuspecting juveniles and in chronic heavy drinkers.

Table 7. General behavioral characteristics at various blood alcohol levels

No. of alcoholic beverages	Blood alcohol level (%)	Effects	Time to wait before driving (hours)
1	0.02-0.03	Slight elevation of mood; mild euphoria; sense of well-being; slight dizziness; some impairment of judgment and memory	—
2	0.05-0.06	Sense of warmth; lowered alertness; mental relaxation; mild sedation; exaggerated behavior; loss of restraints; disruption of judgment; slowed reaction time; decrease in fine motor coordination	1
3	0.08-0.09	Speech impairment; visual and hearing perception impaired; loss of some motor skills; equilibrium reduced; exaggerated emotion; talkativeness; noisiness	2
4	0.11-0.12	Gross motor coordination affected; clumsiness; impaired ability to drive a car; drowsiness; unsteadiness; depression of sensory functioning; mental faculties impaired	3
5	0.14-0.15	Major physical and mental impairment; severe impairment of perception and judgment; unsteadiness and staggering; difficulty in talking	4
7	0.20	Marked depression of sensory and motor capabilities; difficulty in maintaining standing position; visual distortions; poor judgment; confusion; high driving risk	5
10	0.30	Severe motor disturbances; poor comprehension; uninhibited behavior; stupor condition; may vomit; involved in accidents frequently	9
14	0.40	Almost complete loss of feeling and perception; may be unconscious, in a stupor, or coma	
17	0.50	Coma	
20	0.60	Death due to cardiac and respiratory failure	

Uncoordinated behavior is characteristic at 0.10 BAC level. A person driving an automobile with a blood alcohol concentration of 0.10 or higher would be considered driving while intoxicated in most states. If convicted of this misdemeanor, the penalty usually consists of a suspended or revoked license, fine, imprisonment, or both.

At a blood alcohol concentration of 0.15, major impairment of physical and mental functioning occurs. A person's judgment is impaired, and the individual may experience difficulty in standing and walking. With a BAC of 0.15, an individual would be considered driving while intoxicated in every state.

As the BAC increases, greater depression of the brain results. Unconsciousness or coma usually accompanies a BAC of 0.4. If concentrations of 0.5 are reached, the respiratory and circulatory centers of the brain are depressed to where death may result from inadequate blood and oxygen.

Generally these extreme BACs are never reached because the drinker usually vomits or becomes unconscious. However, sometimes when the critical BAC for vomiting (0.12) is reached slowly, the vomit center in the brain becomes depressed and vomiting never occurs.[2] A lethal dose can then be consumed before the drinker passes out, and the individual dies due to anesthesia of the vital centers.

■ METABOLISM

Once alcohol enters the bloodstream, it immediately passes through the portal system into the liver where it undergoes metabolic changes. About 90% of the alcohol that

---

MYTH: I HAVE A HANGOVER FROM SWITCHING DRINKS.

The "morning after" effect of alcohol is not caused by the mixing of drinks. The hangover, in reality, is the adverse reaction of the body to the alcohol consumed the night before. Hangovers are not always experienced after drinking alcohol. The amount and the rate at which beverages are consumed influences whether one will experience a hangover. Hangovers are also more common when the drinker is tired, under stress, or extremely active while drinking.

The symptoms of the hangover usually occur after most of the alcohol has been oxidized. These symptoms include headache, upset stomach, nausea, dizziness, and general weakness. These symptoms are temporary and usually disappear within a few hours after the total oxidation of the alcohol in the body.

The exact causes of the hangover symptoms are unclear; however, some are believed to be related to the accumulation of acetaldehyde in the tissues in the body. Others are explained by other physiological changes. The headache that normally accompanies a hangover is believed to be caused by a dilation of blood vessels in the brain, an allergic reaction to the natural products found in alcoholic beverages, or low blood sugar levels. The nausea and upset stomach have been attributed to the irritating effect of alcohol on the stomach lining.

Remedies for hangovers are numerous—the use of coffee, vitamins, fructose, raw eggs, and alkalizer have all been recommended by people at one time or another. None of these have been proven scientifically effective. The best cure is an ounce of prevention the night before or aspirin and bed rest the day after.

Step 1

$$H-\underset{\underset{H}{|}}{\overset{\overset{H}{|}}{C}}-\underset{\underset{H}{|}}{\overset{\overset{H}{|}}{C}}-OH \quad \xrightarrow{\text{(Dehydrogenase)}} \quad H-\underset{\underset{H}{|}}{\overset{\overset{H}{|}}{C}}-C\begin{subarray}{l}H \\ \\ O\end{subarray}$$

Ethyl alcohol → Acetaldehyde

Step 2

$$H-\underset{\underset{H}{|}}{\overset{\overset{H}{|}}{C}}-C\begin{subarray}{l}H \\ \\ O\end{subarray} \quad \longrightarrow \quad H-\underset{\underset{H}{|}}{\overset{\overset{H}{|}}{C}}-C\begin{subarray}{l}OH \\ \\ O\end{subarray}$$

Acetaldehyde → Acetic acid

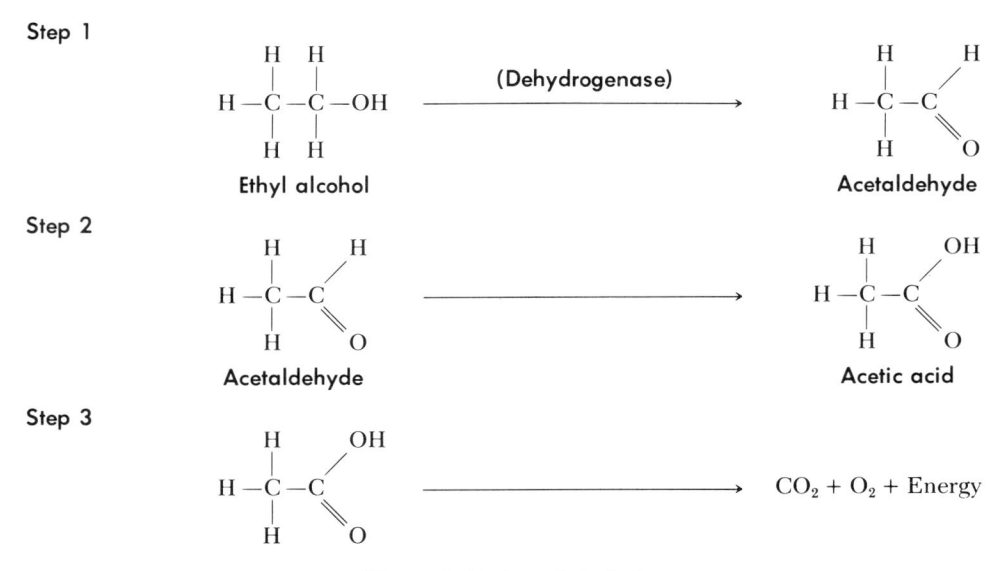

Step 3

$$H-\underset{\underset{H}{|}}{\overset{\overset{H}{|}}{C}}-C\begin{subarray}{l}OH \\ \\ O\end{subarray} \quad \longrightarrow \quad CO_2 + O_2 + \text{Energy}$$

Fig. 8. Oxidation of alcohol.

enters the body is oxidized by the liver. The remainder is excreted from the body through the lungs, kidneys, and skin.

The first step in a three-step oxidation process begins with the action of the enzyme dehydrogenase on the alcohol in the liver. All three steps in the metabolism of alcohol are shown in Fig. 8. Ethyl alcohol is first converted into acetaldehyde, a substance that is toxic to the body and that is partially responsible for the "hangover" symptoms experienced after heavy indulging.

In the second phase of metabolism, the acetaldehyde is further oxidized into acetic acid. This step takes place not only in the liver but also in other tissues and organs of the body.

MYTH: I'LL HAVE A CUP OF COFFEE TO SOBER UP.

Regardless of the stimulant or drug taken into the body, the speed at which an individual sobers up is governed by the liver. Even though the sobering up value of coffee is professed by many bartenders, policemen, and people in general, coffee actually has no effect on an individual's recovery from intoxication. The sobering process is totally dependent on the breakdown of alcohol by the liver.

This process may differ somewhat among individuals; however, it remains constant for each individual person. The use of coffee or any of the other popular methods such as taking cold showers, exercising, or breathing fresh air will not influence the rate at which alcohol is metabolized. Only the passage of time and the work of the liver can sober a person.

Even though coffee does not speed the sobering process, the stimulating effect of the caffeine in the coffee has some benefits. Certainly, a wide-awake drunk behind the wheel of an automobile is better than a drowsy one—if we have to have one at all. Better yet, don't drink and drive.

During the final phase the acetic acid is broken down into water and carbon dioxide. This chemical change where energy is released is known as the Krebs cycle. The energy released is equivalent to about seven calories per gram of alcohol. Since alcohol cannot be stored in the body, the energy produced during metabolism is used immediately, causing other foodstuff ordinarily used in energy production to be stored in the body. This tends to be the cause of large weight gains in heavy drinkers.

The conversion takes place at a rate of about one third of an ounce of pure alcohol per hour. It is equivalent to about three fourths of an ounce of wiskey, two and one half ounces of wine, and eight ounces of beer per hour. The rate at which a person will "sober up" cannot be altered. Despite popular myths, the use of coffee, cold showers, and exercise cannot increase the rate of metabolism of alcohol. Only the passage of time governs the "sobering process." This has practical application in that a person can judge the approximate time he must wait after drinking before it is safe to drive an automobile.

■ EFFECTS ON SPECIFIC ORGANS OR FUNCTIONS
☐ Liver

Continual alcohol abuse can have a lasting effect on the liver. Liver ailments are common among chronic users of alcohol. The most severe of these liver problems is Laennec's cirrhosis. Cirrhosis is an advanced liver disorder where liver tissue is replaced by fibrous tissue similar to scar tissue. The etiology of the disease is unclear,

---

MYTH: ALCOHOL STIMULATES SEXUAL DESIRES.

Alcohol has long been thought to influence sexual behavior by diminishing the inhibitions of the drinker. Small amounts of alcohol are believed to be capable of reducing inhibitions and promoting sexual interest and arousal. However, recent investigations have begun to cast some doubt in support of the theory that the expectancy of the individual, rather than the inhibitory effect of alcohol, is responsible for the increased sexual responsiveness found in individuals after or during drinking.

The expectancy of the individual in relation to alcohol use was proven to affect the perception of individuals.[17] The anticipated effect of various amounts of alcohol, and not the pharmacological effects of the beverage, was found to be the main factor influencing perception.

Physical arousal was also found to be related to expectancy rather than alcohol use.[4] In this investigation, differences in sexual arousal were predicted by researchers on the basis of expectancy and alcohol consumption. The results showed that the subjects who expected to receive alcohol but consumed only tonic water had the same sexual arousal levels as the group who expected and received alcohol.

The expectancy of the subject about the alcohol content of the beverage was again found related to differences in measured sexual arousal. Regardless of the actual contents of the drink, the subjects who believed they consumed alcohol showed greater sexual arousal then the subjects who believed they drank only tonic water.[18]

As a result of these studies, the disinhibiting effect of alcohol is being disputed. It appears that sexual arousal is enhanced or inhibited by the expectancy of the individual rather than the effects of alcohol. Continued research is still needed to determine the definite relationship between alcohol and sexual behavior.

but it is believed to result from nutritional disturbances associated with alcohol abuse rather than from the direct action of alcohol on the liver.

Cirrhosis is believed to be progressive and begins with accumulation of lipids in the liver. These lipids are present in the liver after heavy drinking. Although their functional effect on the liver is unclear, they have been reported to be a cause of sudden fatty liver disease. When heavy drinking occurs over a prolonged period of time, a condition known as alcohol hepatitis may occur. This condition, which is considered more serious than fatty liver, is characterized by inflammation of the liver. As the condition worsens, the size and shape of the liver is altered and its normal functioning is impaired. Eventually liver cells die and are replaced by fibrous tissue. As the degeneration of the liver tissue continues, cirrhosis, the most serious liver condition, develops. With this condition the diseased liver causes the heavy drinker to experience such symptoms as fever, chronic indigestion, abdominal pains, nausea, and loss of appetite. If heavy drinking continues, portal hypertension and hepatic coma can result, or death from extensive hemorrhaging.[3]

Liver damage affects approximately 75% of all heavy drinkers. About 8% of these individuals develop Laennec's cirrhosis. Cirrhosis, including Laennec's cirrhosis, is one of the ten leading causes of death in the United States, and its incidence is on the rise.

☐ Stomach

Gastritis is an inflammation of the stomach lining that can be caused by excessive use of alcohol. This disorder is usually present before liver disease develops and is common among heavy drinkers. The development of gastritis depends largely on alcohol intake.

Alcohol taken in small quantities may tend to improve the digestive process by stimulating the production of gastric juices. However, when taken in large amounts, alcohol acts as an irritant and causes inflammation and damage to the mucosal lining of the stomach. Excessive use of alcohol will eventually cause ulceration and hemorrhage of the stomach lining.

As this condition progresses, the excessive irritation of alcohol causes nerve cells in the stomach to be destroyed. When this occurs, the pain associated with the ulceration and bleeding may not be detectable. In addition, the stomach loses muscle tone, and the churning movements in the stomach cease to function normally. This affects digestion, and nausea and vomiting occur regularly.

☐ Sexuality

The few studies that have dealt with the effects of alcohol on sexual responsiveness indicate that alcohol tends to act as a depressant. Sexual arousal in males has been found to decrease significantly as the level of alcohol in the body increases.[4] Subjects assigned to alcohol and control groups were measured for sexual responses during the viewing of an erotic film. Changes in penile tumescence, a physiological measure of sexual arousal, were monitored. The results demonstrated that increasing blood alcohol concentrations produced decreases in penile tumescence in all the male subjects.

Penile diameter was also found to be affected by alcohol.[5] Changes in penile diameter were used to measure sexual arousal in men who consumed different quantities of alcohol. An increase in penile diameter was found at very low blood alcohol concentrations. Decreases were noticed as concentrations went above 0.025.

Sexual responsiveness was also found to decrease with prolonged usage of alcohol. Large doses were found to cause temporary impotency. Heavy users of alcohol over a long period of time were found to experience permanent impotence even when they ceased consuming alcohol.[6]

The small amount of research that has been conducted on alcohol and sexual responsiveness has included only men. The research suggests that alcohol tends to depress sexual arousal in males. In order to have a comprehensive understanding of the role alcohol plays in human sexuality, more research involving both male and female subjects is needed.

☐ Cancer

Clinical observation along with epidemiological studies have demonstrated an association between smoking and cancer. However, the relationship between alcohol and cancer is just now beginning to come under close scrutiny. The Second Report to Congress on Alcohol and Health[3] reviewed a number of investigations that have found an association between the excessive use of alcohol and cancer. Associations were made between the heavy use of alcohol and cancer of the pancreas, liver, esophagus, and stomach. Geographic studies also correlated the per capita consumption of alcohol with cancer mortality. Beer consumption was found to be associated with cancer of the colon, rectum, breast, and thyroid.

The cooperative role between alcohol and tobacco in the development of certain cancers is also evident. Findings of various investigations have implicated the combined use of alcohol and tobacco with the risk of developing cancer of the mouth, pharynx, larynx, and esophagus.[7]

Increases in the use of alcohol and tobacco have also been correlated with mortality from head and neck cancer. Death from head and neck cancer has increased in the nonwhite population and remained stable for the whites. These differences have been attributed to an increase in use of alcohol and tobacco among the nonwhite population, while it has remained constant among the white population.[8]

☐ Sleep

Instrumental analysis of patterns of sleep indicates that there are two kinds of sleep. One kind is characterized by rapid eye movement (REM) while the other is characterized by non-rapid eye movement (NREM). NREM sleep occurs in four distinct stages, while REM sleep takes place cyclically throughout the night. Dreaming occurs primarily during REM sleep. Dreaming appears to be a basic biological element of the sleep cycle. Deprivation of REM sleep through the use of certain psychoactive drugs has been found to produce a rebound effect in REM sleep. When marked decreases in REM sleep occurred as a result of the use of psychoactive agents, increases in the amount of REM sleep were found on the nights following withdrawal from these drugs.

The research literature concerning the effects of alcohol on sleep indicates that alcohol causes alterations in REM sleep. REM sleep was found to be reduced when moderate amounts of alcohol were consumed.[9] Similar reductions in REM sleep were found in another study using small amounts of alcohol. In this study the loss of REM sleep was not found to be accompanied by a rebound or compensation effect.[10]

However, when REM sleep was examined by breaking the nights into halves, marked suppression of REM sleep was observed during the first half of the night and increases in REM sleep the second half. As larger doses of alcohol were administered, decreases in overall REM sleep were noticed. A rebound effect was also observed following alcohol withdrawal.[11]

When chronic heavy users of alcohol were studied, extreme disturbances in REM sleep were found.[12] Normal REM sleep was found in the sober chronic alcoholic; however, when the alcoholic went through withdrawal, large increases in REM sleep were observed. REM sleep was found to occupy up to 100% of the total sleep time in the alcoholic who tended to experience delirium tremens and alcohol hallucinosis. On certain occasions these alcoholics were found to experience nightmares that would develop into wakeful vivid hallucinations.

☐ Heart

Evidence concerning the relationship of alcohol to cardiovascular disease is inconclusive. Contrasting findings do exist. Some investigations show alcohol having a health benefiting effect, while others demonstrate a harmful effect.

Longitudinal studies concerned with the relation of alcohol to coronary heart disease show that alcohol is not a significant factor in heart attack. The Tecumseh Health Study and the Los Angeles Study both revealed that alcohol was not a risk factor in coronary heart disease. The findings show that the incidence of coronary heart disease for abstainers was the same as for those who were either light or heavy drinkers. Further investigation showed that former drinkers who had stopped drinking were about three times more likely to have experienced a heart attack then the drinker or livelong abstainer. The reason for the higher incidence of heart attack was unclear; however, the suspected poor health of a percentage of those who quit drinking was believed to be the reason for the greater susceptivility to coronary heart disease in the former drinkers.[3]

These findings on coronary heart disease seem to indicate that the use of alcohol does not have a detrimental effect on the heart, leading to coronary heart disease. However, other research demonstrates that cardiomyopathy is related to the consumption of large quantities of beer. Cardiomyopathy, a disease of the heart muscle, is characterized by congestive heart failure, generalized cardiac enlargement, gallop rhythm, and systolic murmur. This cardiac dysfunction related to alcohol has been found to be a frequent cause of death in alcoholics.[13]

These findings on cardiomyopathy are contrary to the findings of the longitudinal studies on cardiac heart disease. Further investigation is needed before the disease concept of excessive alcohol ingestion is fully understood.

☐ Testosterone

Alcohol has been found to produce consistent changes in plasma testosterone levels in males. Testosterone is the most potent sex hormone in males. Testosterone has been observed to influence the sex drive in males. Absence of testosterone due to surgical removal of the testes or low levels of testosterone caused by malfunctioning testes has been found to result in loss of sex drive.

Suppression of plasma testosterone levels was noticed in male alcoholics during chronic alcohol intoxication.[14] In eight out of nine subjects grouped according to baseline testosterone levels, the testosterone levels were found associated with intoxication. During the 12 days of spontaneous drinking, all testosterone levels except one were found to decrease, with the greatest decrease noticed in subjects with abnormally high levels of testosterone.

The same decreases in plasma testosterone levels in male alcoholics were also noticed by another team of researchers.[15] When testosterone levels in alcoholics were studied in an abstinence setting, they were found to be normal. However, during drinking, significant decreases in plasma testosterone occurred.

In dealing with nonalcoholics, no changes in testosterone levels due to alcohol were noticed.[16] During a period of alcohol intoxication, no significant changes in testosterone levels were found in healthy men. However, marked decrease in plasma testosterone did occur during the alcohol withdrawal period.

☐ Pregnancy

> Behold now, thou are barren and bearest not, but thou shalt conceive, and bear a son. Now, therefore beware, I pray thee and drink not wine nor strong drink, and eat not any unclean thing.
>
> **Judges 13:3-4**
> *Angel to Samson's Mother*

Although the placenta acts as a protective filter for a variety of substances, evidence exists in humans and other animals that alcohol rapidly diffuses across the placenta.[19,20] The effects of alcohol on the fetus are not clearly understood; however, several consistent abnormalities in the offspring of alcoholic mothers have been observed.

Infants born to women with severe chronic alcoholism were found to have patterns of altered growth. Low birth weight along with retardation of overall growth and development were noticed.[21]

Similar evidence from other investigations demonstrates similar patterns of prenatal and postnatal growth deficiencies. Eight unrelated children of three different ethnic groups were found to have similar growth deficiencies.[22] Prenatal weight deficiencies and profound linear growth lags were observed. No tendency for postnatal catch-up growth was also noted. After 1 year, the average linear growth and weight gain were found to be 65% and 38% of normal, respectively. These children were also found to have similar craniofacial, limb, and cardiovascular defects along with coordination and motor performance deficiencies.

Five of the eight children had cardiac anomalies, one with an atrial septal defect and three with defective ventricular septums. Growth defects of the fingers, hands, feet, and ears were also found in most of the children. Microcephaly, an abnormal smallness of the head, was noted in seven of the eight children. The growth deficiency of both the head and the brain showed a lack of catch-up growth through early childhood. Performance testing showed the children to have fine motor dysfunction, poor hand-eye coordination, and delayed gross motor skills.

These patterns of altered growth and congenital anomalies were found in another investigation and described as the "fetal alcohol syndrome."[23] In three unrelated cases the alcoholic mothers produced offspring with microcephaly, prenatal growth retardation, and developmental delays. Motor difficulties, along with minor physical anomalies, were also described.

In another investigation,[24] 41 children with fetal alcohol syndrome were studied. These children were found to have prenatal and postnatal growth deficiencies. At birth the deficit of linear growth was usually greater than that of weight. The degree of growth deficiency of the brain, as evidenced by a smaller than normal head size, were common. The catch-up growth rate for these children was not evident whether the children were raised by the alcoholic mothers or in a foster home.

Other anomalies were also observed. Eye deformities and ocular problems were found to exist. Cardiac anomalies, mostly septal defects, occurred in 50% of the children. Skeletal and joint anomalies, cleft palate, and minor genital defects were also noted occasionally.

The current data indicate an association between chronic maternal alcoholism and serious developmental abnormalities in the offspring, described as fetal alcohol syndrome. The risk of fetal alcohol syndrome is estimated to be between 30% and 50% for offspring of alcoholic mothers.[24] Therefore it is critical that women with alcohol problems are made aware of these risks involved with pregnancy. Expectant mothers should be encouraged to abstain from alcohol use during the full term of pregnancy.

■ SUMMARY

Ethyl alcohol, the intoxicating substance found in all alcoholic beverages, requires no digestion. When taken into the body, the alcohol diffuses through the walls of the digestive tract. Some of the alcohol is absorbed in the stomach, but most enters the bloodstream through the small intestine. This absorption process is influenced by a number of factors such as the amount, concentration, and rate of consumption of alcohol, the condition of the stomach and pyloric valve, and the emotional state of the individual.

Once the alcohol enters the bloodstream, it begins to affect the central nervous system. The effect on the central nervous system will depend primarily on the amount of alcohol in the bloodstream in relation to total blood volume, the BAC. The greater the blood alcohol concentration, the greater the depressant effect of the drug on the individual.

The removal of alcohol from the body is governed by the liver. The oxidation of alcohol in the liver is one of three steps in the conversion of alcohol to carbon dioxide, water, and energy. This oxidation or "sobering process" can convert approximately one third of an ounce of alcohol per hour. Therefore time is the essential ingredient in becoming sober.

Continual use of alcohol has been found to have a detrimental effect on various body functions. The most common disorder is gastritis, an inflammation of the stomach lining. Liver damage is the most serious ramification of excessive drinking. Cardiac dysfunction, endocrine changes, and fetal alcohol syndrome have all been found related to patterns of heavy alcohol use. Changes in sexual responsiveness and patterns of sleep also have been linked to excessive use of alcohol.

A thorough understanding of the physiological effects of alcohol on body processes is essential if the consumer is expected to make intelligent decisions about the use of alcohol. This chapter provided the consumer with a background in the general effects of alcohol on the body. The following chapter gives the consumer information on the effects of alcohol on more specific physiological functioning. The consumer will be presented with empirical research dealing with the effects of alcohol on specific behaviors and skills related to aggression, risk taking, reaction, psychomotor performance, and the cognitive process.

REFERENCES

1. Ray, O. S.: Drugs, society and behavior, ed. 2, St. Louis, 1978, The C. V. Mosby Co., p. 70.
2. Leavitt, F.: Drugs and behavior, Philadelphia, 1974, W. B. Saunders Co., p. 47.
3. Second special report to the U.S. Congress on alcohol and health, Rockville, Md., 1975, U.S. Department of Health, Education, and Welfare, National Institute on Alcohol Abuse and Alcoholism.
4. Briddel, D. W., and Wilson, T. G.: Effects of alcohol and expectancy set on male sexual arousal, J. Abnorm. Psychol. **85:**225-234, 1976.
5. Farkas, G. M., and Rosen, R. C.: Effects of alcohol on male sexual response, J. Stud. Alcohol **37:**265-272, 1976.
6. Lemere, F., and Smith, J.: Alcohol induced sexual impotence, Am. J. Psychiatr. **130:**212-213, 1973.
7. Lilienfeld, A. M., Levin, L., and Kessler, I.: Cancer in the United States, Cambridge, Mass., 1972, Harvard University Press.
8. Feldman, J., and Kissin, B.: A case control investigation of alcohol, tobacco and diet in head and neck cancer, Prev. Med. **4:**444-463, 1975.
9. Gresham, S., Webb, W., and Williams, R.: Alcohol and caffeine: effects on inferred visual dreaming, Science **140:**1226-1227, 1963.
10. Yules, R. B., Lippman, M. E., and Freedman, D. X.: Alcohol administration prior to sleep: the effect of EEG sleep stages, Arch. Gen. Psychiatr. **16:**94, 1976.
11. Knowles, J., Laverty, S., and Kuechler, H.: Effects of alcohol on REM sleep, J. Stud. Alcohol **29:**342-349, 1968.

12. Gross, M. M., Goodenough, D. D., Tobin, M., et al.: Sleep disturbances and hallucinations in the acute alcoholic psychoses, J. Nerv. Ment. Dis. **142**(6):493, 1966.
13. Kissin, B., and Begleiter, H.: The biology of alcoholism. II. Physiology and behavior, New York, 1972, Plenum Press, p. 360.
14. Mendelson, J. H., and Mello, N. K.: Alcohol, aggression and androgens, Res. Publ. Assoc. Res. Nerv. Ment. Dis. **52**:225-247, 1974.
15. Farmer, R. W., and Fabre, L. F., Jr.: Some endocrine aspects of alcoholism, Adv. Exp. Med. Biol. **56**:227-289, 1975.
16. Ylirahri, R., et al.: Low plasma testosterone value in men during hangover, J. Steroid Biochem. **5**:655-658, 1974.
17. Marlatt, G. A., Demming, D. J., and Reid, J.: Loss of control drinking in alcoholics: an experimental analogue, J. Abnorm. Psychol. **81**:233-241, 1973.
18. Wilson, T. G., and Lawson, D. M.: Expectancies: alcohol and sexual arousal in male social drinkers, J. Abnorm. Psychol. **85**:587-590, 1976.
19. Mann, L. I., et al.: Placental transport of alcohol and its effect on maternal and fetal acid-base balance, Am. J. Obstet. Gynecol. **122**:837, 844, 1975.
20. Fuchs, F.: J. Obstet. Gynaecol. **72**:1011, 1965.
21. Ulleland, C. N.: The offspring of alcoholic mothers, Ann. N.Y. Acad. Sci. **197**:167, 1972.
22. Jones, K. L., et al.: Outcome in offspring of chronic alcoholic women, Lancet **1**:1266-1271, 1973.
23. Jones, K. L., et al.: Outcome in offspring of chronic alcoholic women, Lancet **1**:1076-1078, 1974.
24. Hanson, J., et al.: Fetal alcohol syndrome, J.A.M.A. **235**:1458-1460, 1976.

6 EXPERIMENTAL EVIDENCE

The empirical studies reviewed in this section form the core of the alcohol instructional material. The studies deal with alcohol as it relates to aggression, muscle relaxation, psychomotor performance, risk taking, driving, and accidents. The intent in presenting these studies is to create cognitive dissonance. This dissonance effect or uneasiness is created when the consumer becomes aware of the true effect of low and moderate amounts of alcohol on specific physiological functioning and behavior. As a result, the consumer may feel susceptible to alcohol-related problems. This feeling of susceptibility is intended to help initiate modification of alcohol-related behavior.

Numerous scientific investigations concerning the effect of alcohol on human functioning appear in the literature. In order to present the most accurate information concerning the psychological and physiological effects of alcohol on the human body, certain criteria were used for the selection of studies presented in this chapter. In adhering to these criteria, only the most scientifically controlled studies were included.

All summaries of studies presented in this chapter used an experimental-control design. This experimental-control design calls for the equating of both an experimental and control group. The experimental group is exposed to alcohol while the control group is not. Observations are then made to determine what changes occur in the experimental group as contrasted with the control. This type of design assures that if external variables other than the effect of alcohol had brought about change, it was reflected in the score of the control group.

In order to adequately determine the effects of the alcohol on the treatment group, the data collected during the experimental stage had to be accurate. Therefore only those studies that used valid and reliable measuring instruments were selected. The use of valid and reliable instruments afforded some guarantee that the data-gathering device accurately and consistently measured what it was supposed to measure under standardized conditions.

When working with human subjects, as in the case of all the following studies, very small and subtle differences between the experimental and control groups can occur. In order to detect these differences, all data were exposed to statistical analysis. This ensured accuracy in measuring the differences between the two groups and facilitated the interpretation of the data.

When examining differences between groups, these differences can result from the effect of alcohol or as a result of chance. Therefore only those studies that report their levels of significance to be 0.05 and 0.01 were selected. Statistically, this means that when the findings are reported at the 1% of the 5% level, there is only one chance out of a hundred or five chances out of a hundred that the differences in the group are due to a chance occurrence. In studies reporting these levels of significance, one can be fairly confident that the findings obtained were a result of the effects of alcohol and not accounted for by chance alone.

■ MOOD AND AGGRESSION
☐ Study 1

> Boyatzis, R.: The predisposition toward alcohol-related interpersonal aggression in men, J. Stud. Alcohol **36**:1196-1207, 1975.

In order to study the effects of alcohol on the interpersonal aggressive behavior of men, 163 men were observed at one of three different types of experimental sessions. At each session either distilled spirits, beer, or soft drinks were served to the subjects. The subjects were videotaped and had their blood alcohol levels measured three times during the course of the experimental session. This occurred during the early, middle, and late part of these sessions.

The subjects were scored by two teams of men on aggressive behavior as observed on the videotapes. The scoring on aggressive behavior was categorized as follows: joking, dramatizing, expertizing, challenging, suppressing, disagreeing, controlling, moralizing, baiting, snubbing, and defying. This system of scoring was partially based on an interaction process analysis.

An analysis of the results revealed several significant differences between the alcohol and nonalcohol conditions. Subjects in the distilled spirits condition were found to be more aggressive than the subjects in the nonalcohol condition during the early and middle part of the sessions.

The distilled spirits group demonstrated more aggressive behavior than either the beer or nonalcohol group late in the session. The nonalcohol group was also less aggressive than the beer group. When the subjects in the alcohol condition were grouped according to their blood alcohol levels, the groups with the higher blood alcohol levels were found to exhibit the most aggressive behavior.

☐ Study 2

> Warren, G. H., and Raynes, A. E.: Mood changes during three conditions of alcohol intake, J. Stud. Alcohol **22**:979-989, 1972.

Twenty college students were measured for mood changes at different blood alcohol levels under the following conditions: social drinking, isolated drinking, alcohol intravenous injection, and saline intravenous injection. Each subject was used as his own control and participated in all four conditions.

In both drinking conditions the subjects drank as much as they wanted from a readily available supply of bourbon and mixers. A 15% solution of ethanol was infused into the subjects during the intravenous condition. The subjects' blood alcohol concentrations were monitored regularly throughout all four experimental conditions.

A psychiatric outpatient mood scale to assess mood was administered three times to each subject during the experimental sessions. The first administration of the instrument occurred before drinking, the second at a medium BAC (0.05), and the third when the BAC reached 0.10. Drinking ceased when this high BAC was reached.

The results showed that significant changes in mood occurred at both the 0.05 and 0.10 BAC. As blood alcohol concentrations increased, the subjects' mood, as reported by the mood scale, changed. The subjects became more depressed, angry, fatigued, and confused. The subjects also tended to be less friendly, vigorous, and anxious. These changes were found not to be different for the three alcohol conditions. The effect of alcohol on mood tended to be less extreme for the intravenous condition than the isolated and social drinking situations.

☐ **Study 3**

> Hetherington, E. M., and Wray, N. P.: Aggression, need for social approval, and humor preference, J. Abnorm. Soc. Psychol. **68:**685-689, 1964.

The influence of aggressive drive and need for social approval on humor preference was investigated under alcohol and nonalcohol conditions. Forty-eight subjects were grouped according to aggressive drive and need for social approval. The subjects were randomly assigned to the alcohol or nonalcohol conditions and given alcohol or a placebo accordingly. The subjects were then given 30 cartoons to rate according to a five-point humor rating scale. Fifteen of the cartoons had been selected for use because of their aggressive themes.

The results of the study showed that the cartoons were rated funnier by the high-aggression subjects than the low-aggression subjects. Subjects with high aggression and a high need for social approval in an alcohol condition rated the cartoons as more humorous than did a similar group in the nonalcohol condition. The ratings of subjects in the other groups tended to be unaffected by the use of alcohol.

■ RELAXATION
☐ **Study 4**

> Girdano, D. A., Girdano, D. D., and Yarian, R.: Alcohol and relaxation, Unpublished paper, University of Maryland, College Park, Md., 1977.

An investigation to determine whether alcohol can actually relax people was conducted at the University of Maryland. Twenty-seven volunteer subjects participated in the study. The subjects were assigned to an alcohol or nonalcohol condition and given an EMG (electromyograph) to determine muscle tension. Immediately following the EMG pretest, all the subjects were given either an alcoholic beverage or a placebo, depending on their group assignment. The alcohol was administered according to the subject's body weight in order to achieve a desired blood alcohol level. The subjects were administered a breathalyzer test to determine blood alcohol concentrations and another EMG (posttest I) 30 minutes after the ingestion of the beverage. The same procedure was repeated to determine blood alcohol concentrations and EMG scores (posttest II).

Table 8 shows the blood alcohol levels and mean EMG scores for all three testings. Blood alcohol levels were found to increase between posttests I and II. However, the mean EMG scores for muscle tension before and after alcohol ingestion for experimental group as compared to the control group were found to be similar. No significant difference in muscle tension was found between the alcohol and nonalcohol group; therefore it was concluded that alcohol did not decrease muscle tension, which would cause a general relaxation.

■ VISUAL AND AUDITORY PERCEPTION
☐ Study 5

> Ehrensing, R. H., et al.: Effects of alcohol on auditory and visual time perception, J. Stud. Alcohol **31**:851-860, 1970.

In this study on auditory and visual time perception, 16 men and 14 women aged 18 to 30 were used as the study group. The subjects were divided into an alcohol and control group and were tested before and after the intravenous infusion of either an alcohol or saline solution. The subjects judged visual and auditory signal duration on a nine category response scale. Blood alcohol levels of each subject were monitored throughout the testing sessions.

The results of the study demonstrated a significant effect of alcohol on time judgment. Alcohol acted in slowing the "internal clock" and increased the time estimates for the experiencing of one second. The implication of the study suggests that alcohol could affect driving by causing the driver to misperceive acceleration and deceleration on time allowances and driving speeds to reach specific destinations.

☐ Study 6

> Wilkinson, I. M. S., and Kime, R.: Alcohol and human eye movement, Trans. Am. Neurol. Assoc. **99**:38-41, 1974.

Ten young people with normal visual acuity were studied to determine the effects of alcohol on speed of eye movement, smooth pursuit movement, and oculocephalic eye movement. Six subjects received alcohol while four subjects were used as the control. Repeated recordings of eye movements were taken before and for the first hour after the consumption of alcohol.

The analysis of the results showed that peak saccadic velocity, the speed at which

Table 8. Mean EMG scores and blood alcohol levels for experimental and control subjects

Subjects	Pretest EMG	EMG I	EMG II	BAC I	BAC II
Experimental group	459.2	440.0	463.67	0.0314	0.0764
Control group	460.33	465.42	480.8	0.000	0.0000

the eye moves from one visual target to another, was reduced by alcohol. After the ingestion of alcohol, the smooth pursuit movement of the eye was also affected. The ability of the eye to follow a swinging pendulum was interrupted and the movements became jerky. The oculocephalic eye movement, which was measured by the subject's ability to keep a fixed gaze on an immobile target, was not affected by alcohol. The conclusions drawn from these results indicated that alcohol's effect on eye movement will contribute to impaired performance on any skill requiring rapid visual perception.

☐ Study 7

Moskowitz, H., and DePry, D.: Differential effect of alcohol on auditory vigilance and divided-attention tasks, J. Stud. Alcohol **29**:54-63, 1968.

The purpose of this investigation was to examine a concentrated-attention or vigilance task and a divided-attention task under alcohol and nonalcohol conditions. The concentrated-attention task consisted of verbally reporting the absence or presence of audio tones. The divided-attention task incorporated the same vigilance task along with repeating six numbers in correct order heard during the test condition.

Ten male graduate students between the ages of 21 and 40 were used as subjects for the study. Each student was used as his own control and tested twice. During one experimental session the subject received alcohol and during the other he received a placebo. The two testing sessions were conducted a week apart. The alcohol was administered to the subjects according to their body weight.

Although alcohol failed to affect the tone detection vigilance task, conclusive evidence was gathered demonstrating the effects of alcohol on the divided-attention task.

Table 9. Number of correct responses by each subject on the 60 trials of vigilance and divided attention after alcohol and placebo*

	Vigilance		Divided attention	
Subjects†	**Placebo**	**Alcohol**	**Placebo**	**Alcohol**
A	52	49	49	49
B	52	49	47	39
C	50	46	48	37
D	45	48	39	30
E	28	30	31	24
F	52	52	53	45
G	52	50	46	40
H	50	51	45	37
I	46	47	43	35
J	45	46	43	35
Mean	47.2	46.8	44.4	37.1

*Reprinted by permission from Moskowitz, H., and DePry, D.: Differential effect of alcohol on auditory vigilance and divided-attention task, J. Stud. Alcohol, vol. 29, pp. 54-63, 1968. Copyright by Journal of Studies on Alcohol, Inc., New Brunswick, N.J. 08903.
†Subjects A to E received alcohol on first experimental session, subjects F to J on second.

The mean performance score on the divided-attention task was 44.5 correct responses (74%). Under the influence of alcohol the mean performance score declined to 37.1 (61.8%). This difference was found to be statistically significant beyond the 0.001 confidence level. This decrement occurred at BAC levels as low as 0.025 (Table 9).

The results of this study offer more evidence concerning the relationship of alcohol and increased automobile accident rates. Driving an automobile is a divided-attention task with the driver monitoring different incoming sources of information. With this divided-attention functioning being affected by moderate alcohol levels, it offers another possible reason for increased automobile accidents under the influence of alcohol.

■ PSYCHOMOTOR PERFORMANCE AND COGNITIVE PERFORMANCE
□ Study 8

> Evans, M. A., et al.: Quantitative relationship between blood alcohol concentrations and psychomotor performance, Clin. Pharmacol. Ther. **15**:253-260, 1973.

Evidence is available demonstrating measurable impairment of psychomotor performance at blood alcohol concentrations above 0.05. This study was conducted to determine the threshold blood alcohol concentration that would produce measurable impairment on psychomotor performance. The following blood alcohol levels were examined: 0.025, 0.05, 0.075, and 0.10.

Fifteen male medical and graduate students were used as subjects in the study. Each subject was studied five times at each of the five different blood alcohol levels. One testing session was conducted each week and the alcohol was administered using a double-blind procedure. A breathalyzer was used at selected intervals during the testing to determine blood alcohol levels.

The subjects were tested on psychomotor performance, stability of stance, and mental performance. The psychomotor performance tests featured an oscilloscope trace and a steering mechanism that were operated in response to stimuli. The stability of stance was assessed by means of a device that measured the subject's balance-seeking behavior. Mental performance was measured by nine short tests involving forward and reverse reading, reverse counting, addition and subtraction problems, and problems involving addition and subtraction with mental addition of an assigned number.

The results showed that a linear relationship existed between performance impairment and blood alcohol levels. As blood alcohol levels increased, psychomotor impairment was observed on most of the tests involved. At 0.07 BAC, significant increases in scores on the selected tests were observed for 11 of the 14 subjects. All subjects showed impairment on most of the tests at the 0.08 BAC level. Very small amounts of alcohol produced stability impairment. As blood alcohol levels increased, significant decreases in stability of stance were noticed and mental performance decreased in six of the nine tests.

Study 9

Idestrom, C.-M., and Cadenius, B.: Time relations of the effects of alcohol compared to placebo, Psychopharmacologia **13**:189-200, 1968.

The effects of small doses of alcohol on simple psychomotor and perceptual tasks were studied. Thirty-one male students were administered two different doses of alcohol or a placebo in random order on three different occasions. Blood alcohol levels and selected psychomotor and perceptual tasks were evaluated before and 30, 60, and 90 minutes after ingestion of alcohol or the placebo. The blood alcohol levels examined were 0, 0.02, and 0.10. The battery of tests included (1) choice reaction time—time reaction to one of a group of stimuli; (2) bimanual hand coordination—movement of a stylus along a designated area by the use of two diagonal acting controls (similar to an Etch-A-Sketch); (3) critical fusion—adjustment of a light until a flicker results; (4) standing steadiness—measures the anterior-posterior and lateral balance-seeking movements; (5) tapping speed—touching right and left electrodes on command; and the (6) Bourdon's test—marking designated letters appearing in a text as quickly as possible.

Impaired performance was noticed on almost all the tests after the highest dose was administered. The peak effects of alcohol were noticed 30 to 60 minutes after ingestion. Both choice reaction time and bimanual hand coordination were significantly impaired after the low dose of alcohol. No impairment was observed after the administration of the placebo.

Study 10

Sideu, F. R., and Pless, J. E.: Ethyl alcohol: blood levels and performance decrements after oral administration to man, Psychopharmacologia **19**:246-261, 1971.

Twenty-six young male subjects were used to examine the effects of various blood alcohol levels on a battery of performance tests. The tests included (1) cognitive performance—a series of addition problems; (2) a time estimation task—the estimation of a designated time interval; and (3) hand-eye coordination test—centering a spot of light by movement of a control stick. The subjects were tested in five groups with only one group receiving a placebo. The subjects receiving alcohol were given doses ranging from 0.5 to 2 mg/kg of alcohol.

The analysis of the results showed alcohol-induced impairment on the test, with the greatest amount of impairment noted on the hand-eye coordination task. The decrement on hand-eye coordination was found to be strongly related to the blood alcohol levels. Impairment was still noted at very low blood alcohol levels. The scores on the other two tests showed less impairment even at relatively high blood alcohol levels. Maximal effects were noted about 60 minutes after the ingestion of the alcohol.

Study 11

Moskowitz, H., and Burns, M.: Alcohol effects on information processing time with an overlearned task, Percept. Mot. Skills **37**:835-839, 1973.

Evidence from other investigations suggests that alcohol impairs performance by

64 COGNITIVE PHASE

slowing the processing of information by the brain. The speed of processing of information is affected by task demand. This study attempted to measure the relationship between alcohol and task demand and its effect on reaction times.

A group of twenty male subjects participated in two test sessions. Half of the group received the control treatment on the first session and the alcohol treatment on the second. The alcohol was administered according to the body weight of each. Testing began 30 minutes after the ingestion of alcohol to allow for peak blood alcohol levels.

The testing procedure called for the subjects to name visually displayed numbers as quickly as possible. They were tested on six conditions. A condition could contain either 1, 2, 4, 8, 16, or 32 possible numbers or, in information theory terms, 0, 1, 2, 3, 4, or 5 bits of uncertainty (i.e., for 1 bit of uncertainty the stimulus pool contained the number 1 or 2). Half the group started with 0 bits of uncertainty and worked up to 5 bits while the other group worked in the reverse order.

Fig. 9 shows the comparison between the alcohol and the control group for responding time. Alcohol clearly increases response latency; however, it was not related to the number of bits of information. Alcohol increased response latencies by about the same amount regardless of the number of bits of uncertainty.

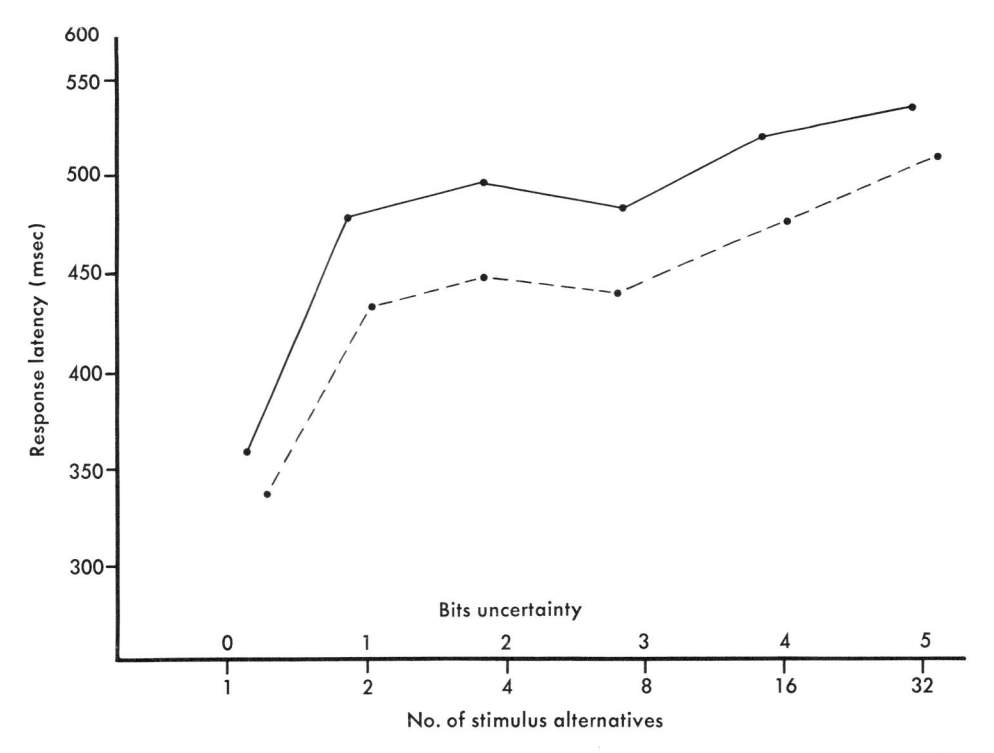

Fig. 9. Nixie light response latencies: control and alcohol treatments. (Reprinted with permission of authors and publisher from Moskowitz, H., and Burns, M. M.: Alcohol effects on information processing time with an overlearned task, *Percept. Mot. Skills* 37:838, 1973, Fig. 1.)

☐ **Study 12**

    Boyd, E. S., et al.: A psychomotor test to demonstrate a depressant action of alcohol, J. Stud. Alcohol **23:**34-39, 1962.

Three consecutive classes of medical students were tested to determine the depressant effects of alcohol on psychomotor performance. The subjects were tested on reaction time modified by the elements of choice and of memory. Each student was tested three times: two predrug tests and one postdrug test. In this way the subjects could be used as their own control.

The classes of subjects were divided into three groups: placebo, 30 ml of alcohol, and 45 ml of alcohol. A double-blind procedure was used to administer the alcohol. No attempt was made to give alcohol according to body weight or to determine the blood alcohol levels of the subjects.

The results of the testing demonstrated a 14% increase in response time after the ingestion of 45 ml of alcohol.

■ REACTION AND CHOICE REACTION TIME
☐ **Study 13**

    Young, J. R.: Blood alcohol concentration and reaction time, J. Stud. Alcohol **31:**823-831, 1970.

This experiment was designed to determine the effects of various blood alcohol levels on reaction time. In order to use the subjects as their own control, the ten participants were tested exactly the same on two separate occasions. During one session they received a placebo and on the other an alcoholic beverage.

The experimental procedure began with a series of practice trials to eliminate a warm-up or practice effect. Five minutes after alcohol was ingested the subject's reaction time was tested and a blood sample taken to determine blood alcohol levels. The same procedure was continued two more times until all the alcohol had been consumed. The taking of blood samples and reaction time continued at $^3/_4$, $1^1/_4$, 2, 3, and $3^1/_2$ hours after the last ingestion of alcohol. The amount of alcohol administered was determined by the weight of the subject.

The findings of the study revealed that simple reaction time was reduced significantly after the ingestion of alcohol. Reaction time was also noted to become less dependent on blood alcohol level with the passage of time. Normal reaction time performance was regained faster than if it were directly related to BAC.

☐ **Study 14**

    Huntley, M. S.: Influence of alcohol and stimulus response uncertainty upon spatial localization time, Psychopharmacologica **27:**131-140, 1972.

Choice reaction time of nine male volunteer subjects between 21 and 30 years of age was studied in three sessions during a 3-day period. A single beverage containing either beer, ethanol, or a placebo was consumed on each of these 3 days. In the two

Table 10. Median reaction times in milliseconds for each treatment combination and absolute and percentage (differences between two beverage treatments for each uncertainty condition)

Uncertainty condition	Beverage		Difference	
	Placebo	Alcohol	Absolute	%
1	478.8	475.6	3.2	0.6
2	606.9	654.8	47.9	7.9
3	814.1	915.6	101.5	12.5

From Huntley, M. S.: Influence of alcohol and stimulus and response uncertainty upon spatial localization time, Psychopharamacology **27**:131-140, 1972.

alcohol conditions the alcohol was administered according to body weight to produce a 0.10 blood alcohol level.

Reaction time was measured by the time between the stimulus presentation and verbalization by the subject. The subjects were instructed to react to a projected dot on a screen by verbalizing a number associated with an area of the screen the dot appeared on. The subjects were tested in three sessions that included three different stimulus response uncertainty conditions. The first condition contained only two locations in which the dot could possibly appear. The second condition contained four presentation possibilities, while the third had eight possible locations.

Table 10 shows reaction time for the blood alcohol conditions as a function of the stimulus response uncertainty conditions. In all three conditions, reaction times were lengthened by alcohol. As the numbr of possible locations for the appearance of the dot increased (uncertainty conditions 2 and 3), the reaction time was significantly greater.

☐ **Study 15**

> Robinson, G. H., and Plebus, W. J.: Interactions between alcohol, task difficulty and compatibility in a choice-reaction task, Percept. Mot. Skills **38**:459-466, 1974.

The effects of alcohol on choice-reaction time tasks of different difficulty and compatibility were examined in this experiment. Thirty male subjects, ranging in age from 21 to 35 years, performed four reaction-time tasks on each of 7 days of testing. The tasks differed in difficulty with respect to the number of response buttons to the various stimulus lights (compatibility).

The subjects were divided into three groups and given alcohol according to body weight, producing the following blood alcohol levels: 0, 0.05, and 0.10. The subjects received alcohol only on the sixth day of testing, while on the other days they received a placebo.

Significant impairment in performance was noted on all the tasks at the higher blood alcohol levels. At the lower levels a significant difference was only observed in the difficult four response reaction time test. Impairment progressed as blood alcohol levels increased. Performance decrement was also noted as the number of alternatives increased or as the assignment of buttons to the stimulus lights became more complex.

■ DRIVING
□ Study 16

> Bjerven, K., and Goldberg, L.: Effects of alcohol ingestion on driving ability, J. Stud. Alcohol 11:1-30, 1950.

The effects of alcohol ingestion on performance in both a laboratory experiment and a practical automobile driving test were evaluated in this study. The road test was performed by two groups of expert drivers on a special track. One group drank distilled spirits or beer while the other served as the control. Both groups performed the road test twice, with the alcohol group being tested both before and after drinking. The laboratory experiment was performed by a portion of the subjects who took part in the practical road test. These subjects were also assigned to a treatment and control group.

In the practical road test, 37 subjects were divided into two series: 14 subjects to be tested with beer and 23 subjects to be tested with distilled spirits. These subjects were then divided into an alcohol and control group. The alcohol group was administered either the distilled spirits or beer according to body weight to achieve the desired blood alcohol levels. All subjects were tested before any beverage was consumed and again 40 to 60 minutes after the consumption of alcohol. The subject's driving ability was assessed by the use of the following six different tests: (1) garage test—driving out of a garage; (2) steering forward test—knocking down three blocks with the front wheels; (3) steering backward test—backing up onto a board; (4) turning on a road test—completing a three-point turn; (5) starting test—driving out of a sand box; (6) parking test—back parking in a confined area.

Nineteen of the subjects from the road test participated in a laboratory test. The subjects were tested on a flicker test (distinguishing a flickering light) and a blink test (determining the stimulus necessary to elicit a blink reflex). Both an alcohol and control group were used in the laboratory test.

The results of both the practical road test and the laboratory test demonstrated the serious impairment caused by alcohol use. Threshold impairment of driving ability was found to occur at a blood alcohol level of 0.035 to 0.04. Deterioration in driving performance of between 25% and 30% was observed after the subjects had three or four bottles of beer containing 4% alcohol by volume. The driving ability of the comparison group improved by 20% from the first to the second testing.

In the laboratory the 32.4% impairment on the flicker test and the 35% impairment on the blink test corresponded to the road impairment of 32.7%. This impairment occurred at an average blood alcohol level of 0.056. Threshold impairment was observed at 0.04 for the flicker test and 0.05 on the blink test. No performance changes in either of the two tests were noticed for the control group.

The agreement in results of the tests indicates that alcohol causes considerable impairment and is a causative factor in traffic accidents. The threshold impairment levels demonstrate that alcohol is involved in accidents at even very low blood alcohol levels. Blood alcohol levels of 0.035 to 0.04 impair driving ability, and at 0.04 to 0.06 BAC as much as 30% impairment occurs.

> **MYTH:** I DRIVE BETTER AFTER A FEW DRINKS.
>
> When an individual drinks alcohol, the ability to mentally process incoming stimuli is slowed. As blood alcohol levels increase, deterioration in reaction time, psychomotor performance, and coordination progressively increases. Speed of eye movement and auditory and visual perception are also diminished. The ability to steer an automobile, monitor several sources of information at one time, and make appropriate decisions all deteriorate. These combined pharmacological effects of alcohol have been proven to diminish an individual's ability to drive an automobile by as much as 30% after consuming only three to four alcoholic beverages. Do you still believe you drive better?

☐ **Study 17**

    Buikhuisen, W., and Jongman, R. W.: Traffic perception under the influence of alcohol, J. Stud. Alcohol **33**:800-806, 1972.

Two groups of 60 men drivers, matched according to age, driving experiences, and driving ability, were used to examine the effects of alcohol on perception of traffic situations. During the experimental session the study group received drinks containing alcohol while the control group was given nonalcoholic beverages. The experimental groups's average blood alcohol level was about 0.08.

After the drinking session, each subject was measured for perception patterns during the watching of a 5-minute film taken from a moving car. During the watching of the film, the subject was instructed to react as if he were driving the car from which the film was made. The perception data gathered from both groups were compared at the end of the experimental session.

Analysis of the data showed that the sober group observed significantly more of the 86 traffic aspects than the intoxicated group. The 50 sober subjects observed a total of 1,974 traffic aspects as compared to the 1,593 observed by the intoxicated group. The intoxicated subjects were found to fix their attention on the middle of the road and missed observing many of the traffic aspects located to the left or right of the road. They were also found to be more aware of the moving objects and more apt to miss the nonmoving traffic aspects. The perception capacity in relation to complex traffic situations of the intoxicated subjects was also impaired. They were found to miss more traffic aspects that were part of a complex situation than the sober group. In these complex situations the sober subjects were able to distribute their attention more than the intoxicated subjects.

☐ **Study 18**

    Cohen, J., and Dearnaley, E. J.: The risk taken in driving under the influence of alcohol, Br. Med. J. **1**:1438-1442, 1958.

Considerable research indicates that reaction time, coordination, the cognitive process, and driving skills are imparied by consuming even small amounts of alcohol. Alcohol-induced impairment is believed to be a contributing factor in a large number of highway accidents in this country. However, the physical impairment of the driver may not be the only factor involved in alcohol-related highway accidents. A more complex psychological factor, the risk the driver is willing to take under the influence of alcohol, may contribute significantly to the problem.

The aim of this study was to determine the effects of alcohol on risk taking and driving performance. Risk taking was measured by the driver's estimate of success before driving. Driving performance was measured in terms of the proportion of successes of the driver during the actual performance.

The subjects in the study consisted of three groups of professional bus drivers with 12 years of driving experience. Two of the groups were administered different amounts of alcohol, two fluid ounces (0.05 to 0.06 BAC) and six fluid ounces (0.15 to 0.20 BAC). The control group received a placebo. After consuming the liquid, each driver was asked to estimate how successful he would be at driving through two vertical poles of varying widths. The drivers, after having made the estimates, then drove the bus through the poles. The widths of the poles and number of successes of driving the bus through those varying widths were recorded for all three groups.

The results of the study showed that all three groups of drivers were prepared to drive the bus through widths narrower than the bus itself. This resulted in the alcohol-free group being involved in accidents as well as the alcohol groups. However, in the alcohol groups, as the drivers' BAC levels increased, they were prepared to take greater driving risks. As more alcohol was consumed, the drivers were prepared to drive through narrower widths. The alcohol group was also found to have a greater confidence of success than the alcohol-free group. The narrowest width the alcohol-free group would attempt was always larger than the width at which the alcohol group would predict success.

Along with the adverse effects of alcohol on judgment, the performance of the drivers also deteriorated with increased blood alcohol levels. Accidents were found to increase with the greater intake of alcohol. As a driver consumed more alcohol, he became involved in more accidents than the alcohol-free drivers.

■ ACCIDENTS
☐ Study 19

Haddon, W., et al.: A controlled investigation of the characteristics of adult pedestrians fatally injured by motor vehicles in Manhattan, J. Chron. Dis. **14**:655-678, 1961.

This investigation was designed to compare the characteristics of adult pedestrians fatally injured by motor vehicles in Manhattan with those pedestrians who were similarly exposed but not injured. The case group consisted of 50 pedestrians whose deaths resulted from being struck by a motor vehicle. Data on the pedestrian characteristics were obtained through a postmortem examination. This examination included the taking of blood samples to determine blood alcohol levels. In order to obtain information on the control group, 200 pedestrians were interviewed and had breath specimens taken for alcohol analysis at the accident site on a subsequent date. The pedestrian subjects were matched according to sex, exact accident sites, time of day, and day of week.

The results of the study showed significant differences between the members of the case group and the control group members in relation to blood alcohol concentrations. Twenty-six percent of the case group as compared to 67% of the control group showed 0 BAC. Forty-seven percent of the case group had a BAC of 0.5 or higher, while only 16% of the control group had a BAC at this level. At the 0.10 BAC or greater, the case group had 47% in the range as compared to only 8% of the subjects in the control group. The percentages of subjects at the 0.15 BAC or higher for the case and control groups were 32% and 6%, respectively. The evidence compiled concerning the differences in characteristics in this case-control study clearly indicates that alcohol was a contributing factor in the death of these pedestrians.

☐ Study 20

>McCarrol, J. R., and Haddon, W.: A controlled study of fatal automobile accidents in New York City, J. Chron. Dis. **15**:811-826, 1961.

Forty-six drivers of noncommercial motor vehicles fatally injured in accidents were compared with nonaccident-involved drivers found at the accident on a subsequent date. The case group represents those drivers killed during a 12-month period in New York City. Data on each deceased victim were obtained through postmortem inspections or examinations. The examinations included the analysis of a blood sample for alcohol concentrations. The control group was obtained by visiting each accident site on the same day of the week and the same time of day at which the accident occurred and collecting data on the passing motorists. The first six drivers proceeding in the same direction as the case driver were stopped, interviewed, and given a breath test for blood alcohol content.

When various characteristics of both the case and control groups were compared, the greatest difference between the two groups was found in the use of alcohol and blood alcohol levels. Seventy-three percent of the drivers rated as probably responsible for the accident had been drinking, as compared to only 26% of the control group. The most significant finding showed that 46% of the case group had a blood alcohol level of 0.25 or greater and not a single member of the large control group was in this blood alcohol level range (Table 11).

☐ Study 21

>Wechsler, H., et al.: Alcohol and home accidents, Public Health Rep. **84**:1043-1950, 1969.

The purpose of this study was to determine the difference between the level of alcohol in a population admitted to a hospital emergency service for treatment of home accidents from the level of alcohol in a population admitted for other reasons. A sample of 11,644 patients who met the investigation criteria were included in the study. These patients were interviewed on admittance to the hospital in order to obtain a description

Table 11. Blood alcohol concentration of fatally injured drivers dying within 6 hours compared with those of noninvolved drivers at the same accident sites*

	Blood alcohol accident conc. category in mg/100 ml†					Lab. loss; no test; no report	Total
	00	<20	20-99	100-249	250-399		
Cases							
No.	14	0	3	2	15	3	37
%	38	0	8	5	41	8	100
Controls							
No.	165(195)	9(14)	34(34)	9(9)	0(0)	5(6)	222(258)
%	74(76)	4(5)	15(13)	4(3)	0(0)	2(2)	99(99)

*Reprinted with permission from McCarrol, J. R., and Hadden, W.: A controlled study of fatal automobile accidents in New York City, J. Chron. Dis. **15:**811-826, 1961, Pergamon Press, Ltd.
†Cases in which postaccident survival was 6 hours or more have been omitted to avoid the artifacts introduced by postaccident, antemortem metabolic lowering of the alcohol concentrations present at the times of the accidents. However, for completeness with respect to the noninvolved drivers; the figures in parentheses give the data for the drivers sampled at all accident sites, regardless of the duration of survival of the corresponding fatally injured drivers.

of the circumstance surrounding the accident. During the interview a breathalyzer test was administered to determine the blood alcohol levels of the patients.

An analysis of the data revealed a significant relationship between the presence of alcohol and the reasons for admission to the hospital. Twenty-two percent of all the patients admitted to the hospital with home accident injuries had positive breathalyzer readings. When compared with the nonaccident group (8.9%), a significantly higher alcohol involvement was found. Furthermore, all types of accidents as compared with nonaccidents had a higher alcohol involvement; the greatest involvement was found in transportation accidents and in injuries resulting from fights or assaults. Transportation accident patients had 29.5% positive breathalyzer readings, while 56.4% of those involved in fights and assaults had positive readings.

■ ALCOHOL AND PERCEPTION
☐ Study 22

> Verhaegen, P., et al.: The influence of small doses of alcohol on the rate of decision making. In Israelstam, S., and Lambert, S., editors: Alcohol, drugs and traffic safety, Toronto, 1975, Addiction Research Foundation of Ontario.

Three groups, each composed of 12 male university students whose ages ranged from 16 to 28 years, participated in the study. The conditions were placebo, low alcohol dosage (BAC of 25 mg/100 ml), and high alcohol dosage (BAC of 60 mg/100 ml). The subjects's task consisted of holding a circle between two parallel lines on a screen by adapted steering movements. Conclusions reached indicated a strong tendency to deterioration of performance in the information processing task at BACs between 50 and 60 mg/100 ml. People under the influence of alcohol at doses of 60 mg/100 ml, and for the older subjects at 25 mg/100 ml, became slower in handling situations that require swift changes in their response choices.

■ ALCOHOL AND DRIVING SKILLS
☐ Study 23

> Mortimer, R. G., and Sturgis, S. P.: Effects of low and moderate levels of alcohol on steering performance. In Israelstam, S., and Lambert, S., editors: Alcohol, drugs, and traffic safety, Toronto, 1975, Addiction Research Foundation of Ontario.

Eighteen subjects (eight females, ten males) were randomly assigned by sex to either placebo or alcohol treatment groups. Subjects had approximately 10 years of driving experience and were on the average in their late twenties. Tests were conducted using a driving simulator. Findings showed that alcohol (BAC 0.07 to 0.10) affected the cue structure used by drivers for path control of the vehicle. There was a reduction in their sensitivity to yaw rate and heading angle cues. Drivers under the influence of alcohol changed their information processing strategy. The mean lateral position error was found by an analysis of variance to be significantly greater at 0.10 BAC than in the placebo condition.

■ SUMMARY

Alcohol has been found to affect human functioning. After examination of the experimental research, noticeable changes in both psychological and physiological functioning were observed after the consumption of alcohol.

Psychological testing showed that subjects tended to be more depressed, angry, and aggressive after consuming alcohol. When the subjects' anxiety states and muscle tension were examined, they were found to be the same whether the subjects used alcohol or not.

Physiologically, alcohol was found to impair performance on human eye movement and affect auditory and visual time perception. Decrements in cognitive processing, psychomotor performance, reaction time, and choice reaction time were observed at moderate blood alcohol levels. When actual driving skills of subjects were studied in relation to alcohol use, impairment was noted to be as much as 30% at moderate blood alcohol concentrations. In studies concerned with home accidents and fatal pedestrian and automobile accidents, alcohol was found to be the major contributing factor.

The empirical information presented in this chapter should enable the consumer to preserve alcohol as a nondestructive part of life. The consumer should have enough information about alcohol to make a mature decision as to whether or not to drink. If a decision to drink is made, the consumer should be knowledgeable enough to drink in a responsible manner. The consumer should be able to differentiate between responsible and irresponsible behavior following the use of alcohol. Hopefully the consumer will be aware of the risks involved with drinking and develop a sense of responsibility for personal welfare and the welfare of others. Ideally, with the information that has been acquired, the consumer should be able to use alcohol without incurring any of the liabilities normally associated with it.

Part III

AFFECTIVE PHASE

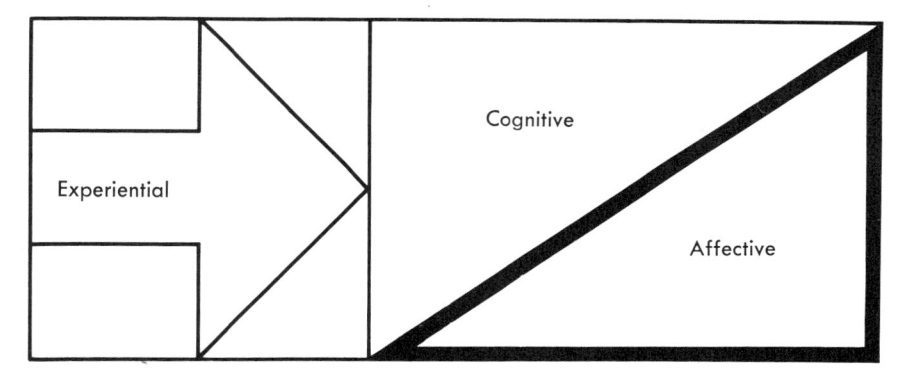

Schema for activated health education.

7 AFFECTIVE DOMAIN

Activated alcohol education is designed to have a positive impact on alcohol behavior. Experiential and cognitive presentations provide a framework in which personal behavior may be examined. Affective education enables consumers to individualize instruction by focusing on motivation and values.

Alcohol is a drug of affect; that is, it influences an individual's internal disposition, attitudes, and subjective responses. The use and misuse of alcohol is related to a variety of feelings and emotions. Several studies[1-3] indicate affective motives for drinking. Among the reasons young people most frequently report for drinking are celebrating, being polite in not refusing, and being friendly. Others drink for relief of tension, to get high, to be a part of the crowd, and to increase self-confidence. Also mentioned are drinking to relieve loneliness and anger as well as to reduce inhibitions and to experience fellings. These motives are in the affective domain. (Note that alcohol myths are involved.) Alcohol behavior has its basis in feelings. Affective instruction regarding alcohol facilitates behavioral decisions based on feelings.

Affective instruction assists individuals in acknowledging their control over and responsibility for personal behavior. The decision to drink should be founded on attitudes that have been adopted as a result of a rational process and that are consistent with life goals. Toward this end, instructional procedures and strategies that involve the affective domain must be incorporated in alcohol education.

The rationale behind affective instruction is that alcohol behavior is personal. Individuals derive their alcohol-related behavior from a variety of personal experiences. These personal experiences are related to the home (Do family members drink? How much? When?), peers (What are group norms?), religion (Does your church advocate abstinence? Moderation?), culture (Do special events require drinking? Is wine served with meals?), and economics (What are your financial priorities? How much spending money do you have?).

Unlike cognitive instruction, which tends to promote rigidity and conformity, affective instruction assumes a continuum of attitudes toward alcohol. Affective instruction affords people the opportunity to solidify their own particular positions on alcohol use. Conflicting positions on drinking practices will emerge, since the issues surrounding alcohol use allow for much discussion. Is abstinence a viable alternative in a drinking society? How much is too much to drink? What constitutes disruptive behavior? The answers to these questions depend on personal experience. People have different experiences and therefore different values regarding their drinking behavior. In order for differences to become broadening rather than divisive, individuals must be willing to accept others' experiences and beliefs while maintaining the integrity of their own. Alcohol attitudes are identified, discussed, adjusted, and confirmed during affective instruction.

Traditional alcohol instruction is cognitively oriented, but current programs are incorporating affective instruction as an integral part. Local, statewide, and national alcohol programs organized to understand and change behavior are including affective alcohol education. The New York State Alcohol Curriculum Guides (NYSACG) for grades K-6[4] and 7-12[5] list affective objectives and suggest program ideas to accomplish same. In the alcohol education program for the junior and senior New York State high schools, students will be made aware of these objectives:

> Be able to seek information so that they can explore their own feelings and attitudes about drinking.
>
> Be able to develop a sense of responsibility for one's individual welfare and that of others in the proper use of alcohol.[5, p.4]

The NYSACG terms the alcohol problem a "people problem." Viewed from this perspective, students' "feelings, values, interests, and actions" are considered. This approach is clearly affective.

The Buffalo Area Council of Alcoholism (Buffalo, N.Y.) in conjunction with the Board of Cooperative Educational Services (Erie County, N.Y.) compiled an entire workbook on affective alcohol education.[6] The following statement is of particular significance with regard to the need for this approach: "Our belief is that local curricula should reflect the nature and needs of the community and individual students."[6, p.1]

Following are examples of activities suggested for incorporation into a program:

HOW DO YOU FEEL BINGO
(as related to alcohol)

Italicized words are key words. As each of the sixteen statements is being read, place the key word of each statement into one of the four columns, depending on how you feel about the statement. (You may have to do some rearranging.)

1. How do you feel about *skid-row* bums?
2. How do you feel about *junior* high kids drinking beer?
3. How do you feel about adults who get drunk at a *party?*
4. How do you feel about drinking and *driving?*
5. How do you feel about drunk *women?*
6. How do you feel about an *alcoholic?*
7. How do you feel about parents drinking in front of *their children?*
8. How do you feel about high school children drinking in front of their *parents?*
9. How do you feel about high school children drinking behind their *parents' back?*
10. How do you feel about *policemen* drinking on the job?
11. How do you feel about *salesmen* drinking on the job?
12. How do you feel about drunk *men?*
13. How do you feel about people who will absolutely *refuse* a drink?
14. How do you feel about *pregnant* mothers who drink in excess?
15. How do you feel about *college beer* blasts?
16. How do you feel about parents who give drinks to *5 year olds?*

Very strongly	Strongly	Mildly	No opinion
			.

QUESTION RANKING

Select four volunteers and have them rank sets of three horrible or unpleasant ideas. Rank in order of least minding to most minding. Disclose each ranking and discuss publicly.

Which would you mind least/most?

1. Being an alcoholic?
2. Having cirrhosis of the liver?
3. Having an alcoholic child/parent?

1. Driving while intoxicated?
2. Being arrested for drunk driving?
3. Starting a brawl because of drunkenness?

1. Being hooked on alcohol?
2. Being hooked on cigarettes?
3. Being hooked on downers?

1. Lowering the drinking age to 16?
2. Raising the drinking age to 21?
3. Letting parents decide when a child can drink legally?

SENTENCE COMPLETIONS

Complete each of the sentences; read aloud and comment.

1. When people drink. . .
2. When I drink. . .
3. Drunk drivers should. . .
4. Parents who drink. . .
5. Teenagers who drink. . .
6. Young children who drink. . .
7. Booze is. . .
8. An alcoholic is. . .
9. A drunk. . .
10. Most drinkers. . .

The American Automobile Association has attitudinal goals in its driving while intoxicated minicourse.[7] Local school programs as well as national projects[8] utilize affective activities as integral components of alcohol learning procedures. University centers around the country have developed ongoing alcohol programs with affective emphasis. Awareness programs [9,10] identify value systems or frames that the student uses as an index in determining personal drinking behavior.

The alcohol awareness program at Morehead State University has a threefold approach: (1) Participants become cognizant of contemporary student persepctives on alcohol use and alcohol-related behavior. (2) Participants are exposed to the professional realm of understanding alcohol (i.e., a chemical, mental, and social understanding). The professional understanding and the student perspective are compared. Both views are recognized as distinct and legitimate. (3) Participants formulate and articulate their personal alcohol behavior.

Values clarification and humanistic education are offered in relation to alcohol within the structure of formal courses.[11] Peer alcohol educators are students selected and trained to work with groups of other students in alcohol education programs.[12] The peer educators are chosen on a number of factors that relate to experience with values clarification skills and small group leadership. Pscyhology departments involved in alcohol programs[13] have students working through their own attitudes about drinking and drinkers.

■ PROCEDURES

Affective alcohol instruction focuses on the individual. The traditional instructor-dominated interaction yields to participant interaction with the instructor as facilitator. The instructor is not recognized as the primary information source. Participants are experts on their own attitudes, and the world is their source of information. Affective instruction provides the opportunity for the individuals to investigate their favorite subject—themselves.[14] They are encouraged to discuss their own alcohol-related behavior (what they do during and after drinking).

Affective instruction is characterized by nonevaluative participant-determined behavior. The instructional climate is informal, and persons are organized into small groups to experience affective activities. Affective activities are any of a number of strategies organized to involve individuals in values and feelings examination. Specific suggestions for alcohol-related affective activities are included in this chapter and Chapter 9. The activities are designed to generate honest reactions and feelings about alcohol-related behavior. Individuals may become stressed when confronted with their own alcohol values. The most effective alternative the individuals have to reduce their stress level is to examine, justify, and confirm their position regarding responsible alcohol behavior. During affective activities the instructor encounters the participants to isolate reasons for involvement in dangerous or disruptive behavior. Through facilitation the participants find reasonable behavioral alternatives. Reasonable alternatives can be derived by brainstorming. For example, suggestions to avoid driving home from a party while drunk could include continuing to party, taking a cab or bus, staying overnight, walking home, losing your keys, riding with someone else in their car, having someone drive you home in your car, and waiting until you are sober to drive.

Individuals committed to appropriate alcohol behavior would not be uncomfortable and, in most instances, would assist the instructor with encountering and facilitation.

Values are identified and clarified during affective instruction. Persons make a personal value commitment regarding their alcohol-related behavior or drinking philosophy, which they will adhere to in their individual environments. Internal motivation to include the appropriate behaviors in daily activities is accomplished through personal commitment activities.

■ PRINCIPLES

The affective method of instruction involves learning from one's own behavior, the behavior of others, and interactive behaviors during group activities. Affective instruction integrates cognitive and experimental learning. In order to guide a successful affective program, five principles have been identified that tend to improve facilitation of responsible alcohol behavior.[15]

☐ Principle one: openness to expression and feelings

Successful implementation of affective instruction depends on a classroom atmosphere that is conducive to open and honest communication.[16] This criterion does not appear in lists of behavior objectives in program guides. However, open and honest communication is a powerful factor. Facilitators and participants need to be able to share feelings without threat and to listen with understanding. Persons must be convinced that the instructor is not present to use authority (traditional role) but to yield it (facilitation role). Punishment and aversive control are antithetical to openness and must be relinquished to achieve fuller participation by reducing fear.

Affective instruction encourages people to interact with each other and express themselves freely. Strong feelings should be examined in the light of other people's honesty.[17] Individuals learn about their own feelings and personalities when the instructional climate is open and comfortable. As a result of honest relationships, individuals transfer more of the learning to personal behavior outside of the instructional setting. Children are naturally open; ridicule teaches them not to be so. Affective instruction helps to revive natural openness.

☐ Principle two: nonjudgemental acceptance of feelings

During affective instruction, as participants interact and instructors relate, the communication of feelings is accomplished. Feelings about drinking are neither right nor wrong, good nor bad. Feelings are an extension of oneself, the integration of experience, and the expression of self-concept. No text can teach nor test measure the appropriateness of an individual's feelings. In affective education the facilitator and learners must be certain not to dictate feelings, verbally or nonverbally. Stated another way, all parties must be nonjudgmental.

Those involved in affective instruction evaluate personal feelings in light of their life experience. What a travesty to suggest to anyone that they should not feel the way they do. Since these feelings originated from life experience, one would in effect be asked to deny experience[18]: "If that's what life has taught you, I cannot respect your feelings, the extension of you." Affective instruction seeks not to condemn, humiliate, or stifle. All feelings are acceptable. Negative feelings such as boredom, apathy, or stillness are just as permissible as positive feelings such as involvement, interest, and importance.

☐ **Principle three: relevance to life experiences**

An educational truism states that "teachers do not teach classes; teachers teach individuals." This simple truth is important because our society demands that people are not alike—people are equal but of different heritage. Yet educators have the task of addressing a heterogenous group with a standard instructional package.

Considering this dilemma, theorists suggest that learning be related to the life experiences of the learner. People learn what is relevant to them. All people will not learn the same material. The instructor hopes individuals will learn that which is meaningful, that which is relevant to them. One way to maximize learning is to make the learner the topic of study.[14] Cognitive learning is potentially stifling to creative individuals and worse yet for those with low self-esteem and a history of failure. The instructor rarely can discern what it is that each person should know in order to live more beneficially. The instructor can allow individuals to decide what is relevant and can allow them the liberty to investigate.

☐ **Principle four: risk taking in communication and behavior change**

Affective instruction involves risk taking in two ways. First, risks are associated with communicating on a feelings level. Each person is comfortable on a different level of intimacy. Some consider their internal disposition completely personal and keep it so. Others use the opportunity for encounter to increase self-understanding. The risk of intimacy is rejection, the reward of intimacy is self-knowledge. For every measure of personal input, an equal risk to self-esteem and confidence is counted as well as the potential for greater personal satisfaction.

A second risk is that behavior change occurs when an individual is willing to risk a change of status. In moving from a known to an unknown one incurs a chance of failure. Can I cut off drinks to my drunk friends? Can I limit my own drinking? Persons experience high satisfaction from high-risk changes. Little change involves little satisfaction. Satisfaction gained from risk taking serves as motivation to continue behavior change.

☐ **Principle five: commitment/actualization of new behaviors**

Commitment/actualization is the final objective of the affective domain. The entire affective effort can be evaluated in terms of whether persons are really acting in ways that are beneficial to self and others. This final principle is the means by which instructors can justify the inclusion of affective instruction.

Individuals who are committed to intelligent and self-fulfilling action will perform new behaviors publicly and repeatedly. This completes the activation process in which persons integrate cognition and affective response and adopt behaviors into their daily activities. Actualization is when a person has identified, can understand, and practices a behavior. Actualization occurs when the new behaviors become an integral part of the individual's personal value system. Individuals transmit these values to their families and friends as they affirm their choice.

■ SUMMARY

Alcohol use is consistently associated with affective motivation. The affective domain relates to one's feelings, values, and attitudes. Alcohol education must include not only experiential and cognitive instruction but also procedures that focus on behavioral decision making. Behaviors and attitudes related to alcohol use are identified, discussed, adjusted, and confirmed during affective instruction.

The individual is the focus of the affective instructional protocol. Five principles have been identified to assist the individual in learning from personal behavior, the behavior of others, and interactive behavior. The principles include (1) openness to expression and feelings; (2) nonjudgmental acceptance of all feelings; (3) relevant discussion of the learners' life experiences; (4) risk taking in communication and behavior change; and (5) commitment/actualization of new behaviors.

■ REFERENCES

1. Jung, J.: Drinking motives and behavior in social behavior, J. Stud. Alcohol **38**(5):944-952, 1977.
2. Riley, J. W., Marden, C. F., and Lifschitz, M.: The motivational pattern of drinking: based on the verbal responses of a cross section of users of alcoholic beverages, J. Stud. Alcohol **9**:353-362, 1948.
3. Fallding, H., and Miles, C.: Drinking, community and civilization: the account of a New Jersey interview study, no. 9, New Brunswick, N.J., 1974, Rutgers Center of Alcohol Studies.
4. Alcohol education: a teacher's curriculum guide for grades K-6, 1976, University of the State of New York, State Education Department, Bureau of Drug Education.
5. Alcohol education: a teacher's curriculum guide for grades 7-12, 1976, University of the State of New York, State Education Department, Bureau of Drug Education.
6. Alcohol abuse prevention education—some beginnings, Buffalo Area Council on Alcoholism and BOCES, Erie-Cattaraugus Counties, N.Y., no. 2, 1974.
7. DWI mini-course for high school driver education programs, Safety Research and Education Project, Teachers College, Columbia University, Sponsored by AAA Foundation for Traffic Safety, Feb. 1976.
8. Kimmel, C.: A prevention program with punch—the national PTA's alcohol education project, J. Schl. Health **46**(4):208-210, 1976.
9. Morehead State University, Alcohol Awareness Program, Kit Christensen, Program Coordinator.
10. Indiana University, Alcohol Education Task Force and Program Module, Ruth C. Engs, Chairperson.

11. South Carolina School of Alcohol and Drug Studies, University of South Carolina, Earl Griffith, Director.
12. University of Massachusetts, Training Program for Peer Counselors and Training Program for Peer Alcohol Educators.
13. Rutgers University, Livingston College, Department of Psychology, N. Cross, Jay, Introduction of Alcohol Programs.
14. Greenberg, J. S.: Perceptions of me, Sch. Health Rev. July/Aug., 1974, pp. 44-45.
15. Dennison, D.: A motivational model to modify actual health behavior, contract no. NIH-72-4295, 1972, U.S. Department of Health, Education, and Welfare.
16. Schlaadt, R. G.: Implementing the values clarification process, Sch. Health Rev., Jan.-Feb., 1974, pp. 10-12.
17. Epstein, C.: Affective subjects in the classroom: exploring race, sex and drugs, New York, 1972, Intext Educational Publishers, p. 36.
18. Raths, L. E., Harmin, M., and Simon, S. B.: Values and teaching, Columbus, Ohio, 1966, Charles E. Merrill Publishing Co., p. 36.

8 PSYCHOSOCIAL COMPONENTS

This chapter provides background information regarding the association between psychosocial variables and alcohol health. The process of group dynamics and communication is enhanced. Competence in this area improves the behavioral change process. Additionally, preparation in skills (affective principles) and knowledge (psychosocial research) increases sensitivity and promotes interactions.

Problem drinking is related to psychosocial health. Certain psychological and social factors correspond to an individual's status on the alcohol health continuum.

Problem drinkers can be described in terms of how they view themselves (psycho) and others (social). The psychosocial profile of problem drinkers has been referred to as the alcoholic personality. Research related to an alcoholic personality is inconclusive. However, various correlations between personality characteristics and problem drinkers are noteworthy. The investigation of the psychosocial components of problem drinking provides a direction for etiological inquiry and a focus for preventive efforts and treatment modalities.

Alcohol-related behavior problems are associated with many factors. The literature is replete with speculation regarding the psychosocial components of problem drinking. Some of the more common theories suggest that alcohol serves to reduce anxiety; to escape reality, guilt, or shame; to cope with failure and feelings of hate, bitterness, loneliness, and isolation. Individuals abusing alcohol have been connected to needs to dominate, lack of persistence in work effort, and confusion over parent models. Other problem drinking theories cite guilt from masturbation, erotic sexual drives including sadism and masochism, and oedipal conflicts.[1] Clearly, alcohol behavior problems involve many variables. While individual characteristics account for some drinking behavior, there appear to be general psychosocial factors common to problem drinkers.

The associations between psychosocial variables and alcohol health must be viewed with caution. While a variety of components appear to be strongly correlated with health status, causative relationships cannot be deduced from the research literature. The proportions of a causative investigation become immense when the interacting relationships of all of the elements are considered. Each variable potentially effects alcohol health status directly or indirectly through cumulative action with other variables. Conversely, alcohol behavior may affect each variable in a similar fashion. In fact, the problem of causation becomes so involved that the very concept might be inappropriate. A web of association seems to represent a closer understanding of the actual experience of alcohol users (Fig. 10).

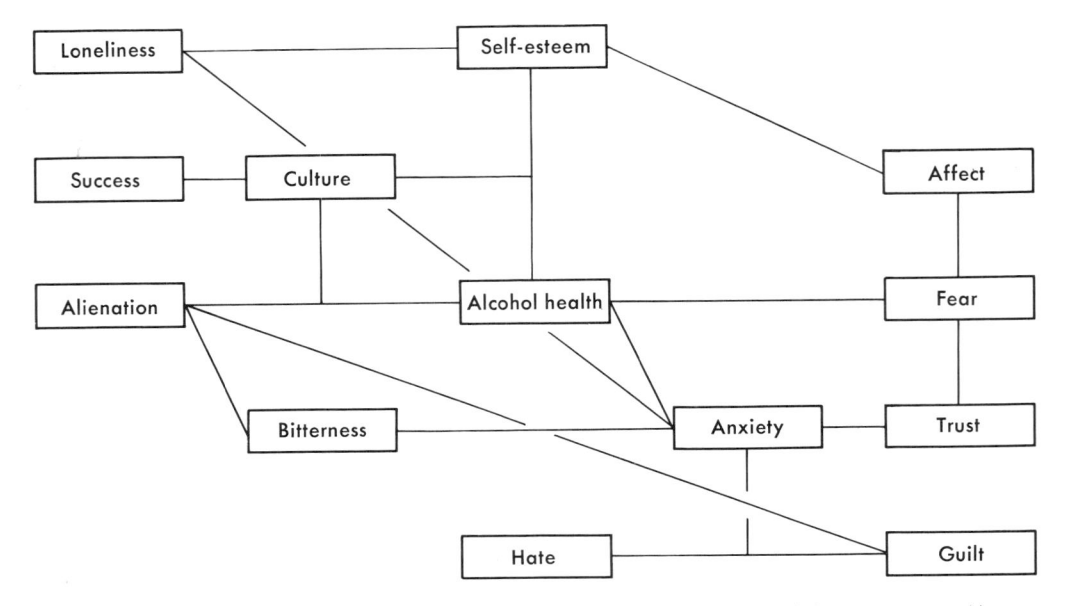

Fig. 10. A web of associations between alcohol, health, and psychosocial components. (Any factor may enter into relationship with any other factor. The web may be drawn to represent the relationships affecting a particular individual. As more components are introduced and relationships discovered, the web quickly becomes a knot.)

The web of association allows for several possibilities:
1. Each psychological and social component may have an independent effect on alcohol health.
2. Combinations of psychological and social components may have cumulative effects on alcohol health.
3. Alcohol health may have independent effects on psychological and social components.
4. Alcohol health may have effects on a combination of psychological and social components.
5. New research findings can be added without disregarding past evidence.
6. The psychosocial web can interface with physical health status.
7. Individual differences can be considered.

Within the web of association, several psychosocial components are consistently correlated with problem drinking in research findings.

■ SELF-CONCEPT

Problem drinkers have demonstrated a proneness to underevaluate themselves.[2] Commonly observations identified low self-concept and sense of inferiority and inadequacy in problem drinkers.[3] Apparently, persons who have negative feelings about themselves exhibit ineffective behavior and problem drinking. In turn, individuals view themselves as ineffective and maintain their low self-concept.

Inadequacy and lack of self-respect are characteristics of problem drinkers. A self-concept scale was administered to male alcoholics.[4] The individuals were volunteers who entered a 60-day alcoholic treatment program. In comparison to a control group, alcoholics perceived themselves less favorably on internal factors. These factors included what the individuals thought they were (identity), how they felt about themselves (self-satisfaction), and what they do (behavior).

Problem drinkers also considered themselves with lower regard than a control group on external factors. External factors related to perceptions of the physical self in terms of body, sex, and the moral and ethical self (i.e., moral worth, relationships with God). Other external measures involved feelings of adequacy and worth in relation to self, family, and friends. Alcoholics were found to be more self-critical than the control group.

Low self-esteem in problem drinkers has been reported in other studies. In a Texas county a group of probationers who had been convicted of driving while intoxicated was investigated.[5] As a condition of probation, the people were required to appear for diagnostic evaluation and referral. Each person completed a self-esteem scale. In addition, persons were interviewed by a psychiatrist and a counselor, both of whom had special alcoholism training. Alcoholics were identified. The distribution of scores on the self-esteem scale indicated that a significantly greater percentage of alcoholics scored at the lower levels (low self-esteem). Also, a significantly greater percentage of nonalcoholics scored at the higher levels (high self-esteem). Further examination of alcoholics' scores revealed that those who had the highest self-esteem were most likely to reject help. Conversely, those with the lowest scores all sought help with their drinking problem.

College students with drinking problems also have problems with self-acceptance. A study conducted at a New England men's college employed members of four fraternities.[6] Two of the fraternities were selected because of their reputation for heavy drinking. Among the data collected by questionaires was the extent of problem drinking, self-acceptance, and self-criticism. The hypothesis that problem drinking is associated with low self-acceptance was confirmed. Those men identified as problem drinkers rated themselves consistently more critically and less self-accepting than did non problem drinkers.

The self-esteem of women alcoholics was found to be lower than that of several comparison groups.[7] One hundred twenty women alcoholics were compared to three groups of similar numbers: (1) male alcoholics, (2) women undergoing treatment for mental and emotional difficulties, and (3) women who have never undergone treatment for alcoholic or mental and emotional difficulties. All of the subjects were English-speaking whites matched on demographic characteristics. Women alcoholics scored lower on measures of self-esteem than did men alcoholics and "normal" controls, but women alcoholics scored similarly to treatment controls. Additionally, self-esteem scores of women alcoholics were negatively correlated with measures of alienation, social isolation, neuroticism, anxiety, and depression.

Table 12. Mean subgroup alienation scores

Alienation (n = 70)	Alcoholics (x = 3.80)			Normals (x = 2.24)		
	Male (n = 49)	Female (n = 21)	Average	Male (n = 43)	Female (n = 21)	Average
Normlessness	2.98	2.23	2.61	2.04	1.98	2.01
Powerlessness	4.60	3.25	3.93	2.37	2.19	2.28
Social isolation	4.76	4.97	4.87	2.49	2.34	2.43
Average	4.11	3.48	3.80	2.30	2.17	2.24

From Calicchia, J. P., and Barresi, R. M.: Alcoholism and alienation, J. Clin. Psychol. **31:**770-775, 1975.

■ ALIENATION

Highly alienated persons tend to adopt the use of alcohol to relieve tensions, anxieties, and the fear of failure.[7] Alienation is a state of estrangement from others. Feelings of powerlessness (my life is out of my control), normlessness (no standards of behavior seem to guide my life), and social isolation (I am alone and no one wants anything to do with me) are associated with alienation. Alcoholics have been found to be suffering from a sense of hollowness and defeat.[8] The unmet power needs[9] and interpersonal contacts[10] also pose problems for the alcoholic. The chance for successful rehabilitation is increased when the alcoholic is less alienated.[11]

Alcoholics experience greater alienation that control groups.[12] Members of an Alcoholics Anonymous chapter volunteered to participate in what they believed to be an attitude survey. A control group was recruited that matched the alcoholic group closely in major demographic variables. An alienation scale was administered to the participants. Results indicated that alcoholics were significantly more alienated than the controls. In addition, on the social isolation subscale alcoholics felt the greatest degree of alienation. Alcoholics ranked the powerlessness and normlessness subscales second and third in degree of alienation, respectively. Sex differences were found in responses within the alcoholic group. Males reported more alienation than females, though both sexes felt equally isolated socially (Table 12).

Teenage alienation and heavy teenage drinking have been found to be related. Studies of drinking by teenagers were conducted in two communities in eastern Massachusetts.[13] The towns were chosen to include a range of socioeconomic groups. Junior and senior high school students were surveyed with an anonymous questionnaire. Among other information, the questionnaire identified alcohol use and personal and social characteristics. The findings revealed that teenagers who drank heavily tended to be alienated from their parents and from traditional values and standards of behavior. Heavy drinkers were not likely to feel close to their families, neither were they comfortable discussing drugs with either parent.

■ PEER GROUP PRESSURE

Persons learn and maintain behavior because of the reinforcement gained through alcohol use. Reinforcement can be physical (i.e., central nervous system responses and addiction processes). Reinforcement for heavy drinking may also be psychosocial (i.e., persons come to expect encouragement from others and satisfaction of needs). Peer group pressure is often mentioned as a psychosocial alcohol reinforcer.

In the study of teenagers in Massachusetts, peer group pressure was associated with heavy drinking. Teenage drinkers are likely to have friends who drink. Drinkers also perceive drinking as widespread among their peers. Heavy drinkers claimed to have several friends who drank beer, wine, and even distilled spirits. As a group, heavy drinkers thought drinking was widespread in their peer group. These findings lend credence to the theory that drinking is encouraged by other alcohol users. The need to secure social support for behavior provides a strong association between the drinking behavior of adolescents and that of their friends according to the results of this study.

Adolescent alcohol use is directly related to support from peers and parents. Questionnaires on drinking behavior were completed by white male high school seniors.[14] The students represented 30 schools in the eastern and Piedmont sections of North Carolina. In these areas the major religious denominations vigorously promote total alcohol abstinence. The percentage of student drinkers varied in proportion to parental approval and best-friend drinking behavior. Among those whose parents opposed drinking and whose best friends abstained, 12% drank. On the other hand, 89% drank whose parents drank and whose best friends drank. The study concluded that the primary source of pressures for adolescents to drink and social support for drinking are found within the adolescent society. These pressures affect the behavior of both drinkers and nondrinkers.

Collegiate drinking patterns appear to be influenced by peer group pressure. A study was conducted to assess the extent and prevalence of intoxicant use among undergraduates.[15] An investigation of the factors associated with alcohol use was also undertaken. The analyses are based on the replies of a mail questionnaire. Significant associations between close-friend drinking, sibling drinking, and student drinking behavior warrant the speculation that strong peer pressure to drink exists. High proportions of social drinkers and occasional drinkers considered all or most of their friends to be drinkers. Likewise, abstainers felt that their friends were also abstainers. Students commonly reported that they had been encouraged by their friends to drink though this was not associated with student drinking patterns.

DOMINANCE

Marital dissatisfaction has been found to be related to heavy drinking, feelings of isolation and depression, and the absence of intimate associates.[16] Excessive drinking and "helling around" were principal complaints of divorced women.[17] In another investigation, wives of couples applying for divorce often mentioned problems related to finances and drinking.[18] Interestingly, in couples in which alcohol is already a problem, alcoholic husbands and their wives generally agree that the major aspect of marital happiness deals with interpersonal behavior.[19]

Alcoholic husbands become excessively dependent on their wives.[20] Although heavy drinking is associated with marital problems, there is a tendency for alcoholic husbands to become dependent on their wives. A series of case studies of alcoholics and their wives revealed that the husbands become inferior in status to the wife.[21] Sexual relationships are no longer satisfactory due to the inadequacies of both partners.

Marriage complicated by excessive drinking continues to raise questions of interpersonal relationships, including the dominance factor. In an investigation of the personalities of alcoholics and their wives, couples completed adjective checklist descriptions of self and spouse.[22] Alcoholic men disagreed sharply with their wives over the degree of dominance. Both partners rated the husbands about the same on dominance and affection. Similarly, wives and husbands agreed on the amount of affection of the wives. However, a significant discrepancy emerged in relation to the degree of dominance-submissiveness attributed to the wives. Most alcoholic husbands perceived their wives to be more dominant than themselves. The wives thought the reverse. These data do not yield information concerning whether husbands exaggerate to rationalize continued excessive drinking or whether wives are minimizing their dominance to appear more innocent.

■ PSYCHOLOGICAL NEEDS

The self-reported effects of alcohol vary at different stages of liquor consumption. Cocktail parties were held at five fraternities at two men's colleges in New York State.[23] In a preparty condition, the evening previous to the party, the men were asked to describe themselves in general. During the parties, under the influence of alcohol, the students were asked to describe themselves at that moment. After the consumption of four ounces of liquor the men described themselves as more self-centered, self-assured, and less inhibited. At the same consumption level, students reported being more concerned with heterosexual matters, more impulsive, and less cautious. Erratic, impatient, and changeable descriptions increased; submissiveness, dependence on others, and reflectiveness decreased.

At higher levels of consumption (six to twenty-eight ounces of alcohol), aggression and autonomy increased. Students were less conscientious and dependable at higher drinking levels as well as being more energetic and spontaneous. In general, drinking self-descriptions contained less inhibitions as action predominated over thought. Both high and low problem drinkers are affected similarly under the influence of alcohol. The changes in psychological components are likely to be normal, expected behavior thus reducing personal accountability for action when drinking. Problem drinkers may be induced to drink heavily and frequently because of the behavior that is allowed when drinking.

A large number of psychosocial variables can be used to explain the variance in alcohol consumption. Neither the psychological nor the sociological variables correlated with problem drinkers can be termed causal. This much is known—drinking is a highly reinforced activity. Internal need satisfaction reinforces drinking behavior as well as external social factors. Alcohol is attributed with the following:

1. Outlet for leisure entertainment
2. Release from tension and anxiety

3. Fulfillment of social obligation
4. Expression of hostility
5. Guard against estrangement from others (i.e., loneliness, separateness, alienation)
6. Facilitates togetherness
7. Reward and punishment system
8. Method of achieving high-level excitement, adventure, and experimentation
9. Form of deceit and self-deceit (forgetting)
10. Way to demonstrate belonging to a group, to adulthood, to self, etc.
11. Aphrodisiac and, more cruelly, a means to reduce free choice in sexual encounters
12. Way to communicate

The list goes on and on. In order to change alcohol-related behavior, values toward alcohol and its psychosocial components must be challenged.

REFERENCES

1. Armstrong, J. D.: The search for the alcoholic personaltiy, Ann. Am. Acad. Polit. Soc. Sci. **315**:40-47, 1958.
2. Connor, R. G.: The self concepts of alcoholics, In Pittman, D. J., and Snyder, C. R. editors: Society, culture and drinking patterns, New York, 1962, John Wiley &. Sons, pp. 445-467.
3. Button, A. D.: The psychodynamics of alcoholism: a survey of 87 cases, J. Stud. Alcohol **17**:443-460, 1956.
4. Gross, W. F., and Alder, L. O.: Aspects of alcoholics' self-concepts as measured by the Tennessee Self Concept Scale, Psychol. Rep. **27**:431-434, 1970.
5. Charalampous, K. D., Ford, B. K., and Skinner, T. T.: Self-esteem in alcoholics and nonalcoholics, J. Stud. Alcohol **37**:990-994, 1976.
6. Williams, A. F.: Self concepts of college problem drinkers, J. Stud. Alcohol **28**:267-276, 1967.
7. Calahan, D.: Problem drinkers, San Francisco, 1970, Jossey-Bass, Inc., Publishers, pp. 83-84.
8. Reinhardt, J. M.: Alcoholism and cultural conflict in the United States, Int. J. Offender Ther. **13**:177-181, 1969.
9. McClelland, D. C., et al.: The drinking man—alcohol and human motivation, New York, 1972, The Free Press.
10. Warberg, K. W.: Some psychodynamic dimensions found among alcoholics, Psychother. Theory Res. Pract. **7**:79;85, 1970.
11. Muller, J., and Brunner-Orne, M.: Social alienation as a factor in the acceptances of outpatient psychiatric treatment by the alcoholic, J. Clin. Psychol. **23**:517-518, 1967.
12. Calicchia, J. P., and Barresi, R. M.: Alcoholism and alienation, J. Clin. Psychol. **31**:770-775, 1975.
13. Wechsler, H., and Thum, D.: Teenage drinking, drug use and social correlates, J. Stud. Alcohol **34**:1220-1227, 1973.
14. Alexander, C. N., and Campbell, E. Q.: Peer influences on adolescent drinking, J. Stud. Alcohol **28**:444-453, 1967.
15. Parfrey, P. S.: Factors associated with undergraduate alcohol use, Br. J. Prev. Soc. Med. **28**:252-257, 1974.
16. Renne, K. S.: Correlates of dissatisfaction in marriage, J. Marriage Family **32**:54-67, 1970.

17. Goude, W. J.: After divorce, New York, 1956, The Free Press.
18. Levinger, G.: Sources of marital dissatisfaction among applicants for divorce, Am. J. Orthopsychiatr. **36:**803-807, 1966.
19. Wadsworth, A. P., Wilson, W., and Borker, H. R.: Determinants of marital happiness and unhappiness rated by alcoholics and their wives, J. Stud. Alcohol **36:**634-644, 1975.
20. Mowrer, H. R.: A psychocultural analysis of the alcoholic, Am. Soc. Rev. **5:**546-557, 1940.
21. Bacon, S. D.: Excessive drinking and the institution of the family. In Alcohol, Science and Society, lecture no. 16, J. Stud. Alcohol, 1945.
22. Orford, J.: A study of the personalities of excessive drinkers and their wives, using the approaches of Leary and Eysenck, J. Consult. Clin. Psychol. **44:**534-545, 1976.
23. Williams, A. F.: Psychological needs and social drinking among college students, J. Stud. Alcohol **29:**355-363, 1968.

9 GROUP ACTIVITIES

Affective alcohol instruction encourages individuals to clarify values, solidify positions, and express feelings regarding drinking behavior. The instructor's task is to structure the learning environment in such a way that the learners' interaction will facilitate the achievement of affective objectives.[1] The procedures in cognitive learning, lecturettes, discussions, and recitation complement the instructional objectives of information dissemination. Similarly, affective procedures—process activity, gaming situation, and values clarification—are designed to facilitate alcohol-related decision making.

Alcohol instruction should utilize affective activities to integrate experiential and cognitive learning. However, affective activities have not been shown to effect significant changes in cognitive learning,[2] but research indicates that values and attitudes have been changed as a result of games.[3,4] In affective instruction the attitudinal changes can be combined with knowledge and experience learning to effect positive differences in drinking behavior.

The instructor should be familiar with a variety of activities. The activities should be used at appropriate times in the instructional protocol. Poorly prepared affective activities will fail to generate the participation, learning, and integration desired. Planning procedures for traditional presentations should be employed for affective activities. Participants as well as instructors are provided with all the information in keeping with an open and honest instructional climate. Activities are arranged from least to most involved.

■ MORE THAN HELLO EXERCISE
☐ Purpose

Affective instruction is dependent on trust built through close interpersonal relations. Personal introductions in traditional education focus on names, occupation, and life situation. The emphasis in affective introductions is personal uniqueness (i.e., likes and dislikes, feelings, attitudes, and outlooks). Participants concentrate on topics such as what makes them laugh and cry, who they are, and what are their life goals. Trust involves a sharing of one's internal self, not a review of one's environment, and external self.

☐ Principles

Openness, risk taking

Procedures

1. Participants pair themselves with someone they do not know.
2. Each participant introduces himself/herself in terms of internal self.
3. After participants have had an opportunity to become acquainted, pairs form into groups of four with others they do not know.
4. Again the purpose of the grouping is to provide the chance for participants to get to know each other. This time, instead of introducing oneself, partners of the original pairs introduce each other to the new pair.
5. If time permits, reform again with groups of eight. Participants introduce someone of the second pair to the two new pairs.

■ FIRST IMPRESSIONS EXERCISE

Purpose

Open and honest interaction among participants facilitates learning and knowledge transfer. However, participants may be reluctant to share affective reactions with others if such reactions could be construed negatively or derogatorily. This exercise helps participants understand the hidden deceptions in an area as elementary as first impressions.

Principles

Openness, risk taking

Procedures

1. Participants form groups of four and select a spokesperson for the group.
2. Beginning with the spokesperson and moving counterclockwise, each person tells in a word the first impression they had of each member of the group.
3. When all the groups have had an opportunity to complete the round, the spokesperson announces the words used to describe first impressions in the group.
4. The spokesperson for each group is asked to name any of the comments that made people feel uncomfortable.
5. The groups are asked to formulate a list of words describing their first impressions of the instructor, and the spokesperson reports these characteristics.
6. In the following form the instructor categorizes each word on the chalkboard according to whether the comments created a comfortable or uncomfortable feeling.

Comfortable	Uncomfortable

7. The instructor leads a discussion on why participants are generally unwilling to share uncomfortable comments with each other but are willing to do so with the instructor.

Instructor ends by indicating that in an open and honest instructional climate one is more likely to learn from others and transfer knowledge as well as be more satisfied with the experience.

■ ALCOHOL EDUCATION RELEVANCY EXERCISE
☐ Purpose

Motivation and interest in instructional activity increases when individuals consider alcohol education relevant. Similarly, personal involvement deepens when individuals participate in determining instructional objectives. In the initial phase of an alcohol program, the instructor should be open to suggestions from the participants concerning the inclusion of meaningful content and activity. This exercise provides the opportunity for participants to direct the instructional process toward that which is relevant.

☐ Principles

Relevance, openness

☐ Procedures

1. Participants form groups of three or four members.
2. Participants discuss within the small groups their concerns and expectations of alcohol education.
3. On a scale of one to ten, where one represents no interest and ten represents highest interest, participants rate themselves privately according to how interested they are in alcohol-related study.
4. Groups average the scores of the members and report the mean score to the instructor.
5. The instructor accepts the scores and asks for suggestions for increasing interest.

■ ALCOHOL CONCERN EXERCISE
☐ Purpose

The focus of affective alcohol instruction is the behavior of the participants. Behavior change can only be effected if instruction centers on personal drinking practices. This exercise is designed to allow the participants to quantify their contributions in the total disruptive behavior of the class. Those who have significantly added to the statistics will feel the most uncomfortable. Participants will understand that in order to lower the class total each person must decrease involvement in disruptive activity.

☐ Principles

Nonjudgmental, openness

☐ Procedures

1. The instructor compiles the raw scores of all the participants on the Alcohol Behavior Inventory for all of the frequency, amount, and disruptive behavior items.
2. Participants form groups of three or four members.

96 AFFECTIVE PHASE

3. Participants are presented with the scores of drinking behavior.
4. Participants in small groups discuss their reactions to the information on drinking behavior.
5. On a scale of one to ten, where one represents no concern and ten represents highest concern, participants rate themselves privately according to how concerned they are about the information on drinking behavior.
6. Groups average the scores of the members and report the mean scores to the instructor.
7. The instructor accepts the scores and summarizes participant concern.

■ "FEELINGS" WORD DESCRIPTION EXERCISE
☐ Purpose

Verbal participant feedback is essential in the instructional evaluation process (i.e., determining the effectiveness of activities and procedures). Reactions to experiential activity and cognitive presentations involve participant feelings. Individuals frequently have difficulty naming their feelings. Therefore a list of "feelings" words is included to facilitate expression of feelings. The list should not be limiting but merely suggestive of many possible feelings. This activity may be conducted and repeated as the instructor recognizes the need for feedback.

☐ Principles

Nonjudgmental, relevance, openness

☐ Procedures

1. Participants are provided with the following list of "feelings" words:

accepted	demoralized	horrified	respected
adventuresome	depressed	impish	responsible
amazed	disgusted	inadequate	restrained
ambivalent	embarrassed	indebted	satisfied
angry	energetic	inspired	scared
annoyed	enthusiastic	jovial	sneaky
antagonized	envious	joyful	stimulated
apathetic	euphoric	lonely	strong
benevolent	foolish	loving	superior
boastful	frantic	mad	sympathetic
bored	free	nervous	tense
buoyant	frenzied	noble	thrilled
clumsy	frightened	ornery	tired
cocky	frustrated	overwhelmed	triumphant
confused	generous	oppressed	unique
controlled	grateful	pressured	victorious
convivial	guilty	proud	weak
defeated	happy	refreshed	worthless
dejected	healthy	relieved	

2. Participants will write three words that describe their feelings about the alcohol instructional experiences designated by the instructor.

3. Participants form groups of three or four members to discuss their three word descriptions.
4. Groups compile a list of words used to describe the feelings of their group members.
5. Each group will share the words with the other groups and the instructor.
6. The instructor will list the words and the participants will categorize them according to whether they express negative or positive feelings.
7. The "feelings" words will be analyzed by the instructor to determine the overall feelings about the instructional procedures.

■ GAMES PEOPLE PLAY EXERCISE
☐ Purpose

Participants in affective instruction investigate reasons for drinking behavior. Alcohol use may be attributable to a variety of motivations. Gaming theory provides an alternate method of critiquing drinking practices. Participants discover the applicability of this method of behavior analysis to their own drinking behavior.

☐ Principle

Openness

☐ Procedures

1. Participants are asked to read the following quaternum from the book *Games People Play** by Eric Berne.

    Thesis

    In game analysis there is no such thing as alcoholism or "an alcoholic," but there is a role called the Alcoholic in a certain type of game. If biochemical or physiological abnormality is the prime mover in excessive drinking—and that is still open to some question—then its study belongs in the field of internal medicine. Game analysis is interested in something quite different—the kinds of social transactions that are related to such excesses. Hence the game "Alcoholic."

    In its full flower this is a five-handed game, although the roles may be condensed so that it starts off and terminates as a two-handed one. The central role is that of the Alcoholic—the one who is "it"—played by White. The chief supporting role is that of Persecutor, typically played by a member of the opposite sex, usually the spouse. The third role is that of doctor who is interested in the patient and also in drinking problems. In the classical situation the doctor successfully rescues the alcoholic from his habit. After White has not taken a drink for six months they congratulate each other. The following day White is found in the gutter.

    The fourth role is that of the Patsy, or Dummy. In literature this is played by the delicatessen man who extends credit to White, gives him a sandwich on the cuff and perhaps a cup of coffee, without either persecuting him or trying to rescue him. In life this is more frequently played by the wife who does not understand him. In this aspect of the game, White is required to account in some plausible way for his need for money—by some project in which both pretend to believe, although they know what he is really going to spend most of

---
*From *Games People Play*, by Eric Berne, M.D. Copyright © 1964 by Eric Berne. Reprinted by permission of Random House, Inc.

the money for. Sometimes the Patsy slides over into another role, which is a helpful but not essential one: the Agitator, the "good guy," who offers supplies without even being asked for them: "Come have a drink with me (and you will go downhill faster)."

The ancillary professional in all drinking games is the bartender or liquor clerk. In the game "Alcoholic" he plays the fifth role, the Connection, the direct source of supply who also understands alcoholic talk, and who in a way is the most meaningful person in the life of an addict. The difference between the Connection and the other players is the difference between professionals and amateurs in any game: the professional knows when to stop. At a certain point a good bartender refuses to serve the Alcoholic, who is left without any supplies unless he can locate a more indulgent Connection.

In the initial stages of "Alcoholic," the wife may play all three supporting roles: at midnight the Patsy, undressing him, making him coffee and letting him beat up on her; in the morning the Persecutor, berating him for the evil of his ways; and in the evening the Rescuer, pleading with him to change them. In the later stages, due sometimes to organic deterioration, the Persecutor and the Rescuer can be dispensed with, but are tolerated if they are also willing to act as sources of supply. White will go to the Mission House and be rescued if he can get a free meal there; or he will stand for a scolding, amateur or professional, as long as he can get a handout afterward.

Present experience indicates that the *payoff* in "Alcoholic" (as is characteristic of games in general) comes from the aspect to which most investigators pay least attention. In the analysis of this game, drinking itself is merely an incidental pleasure having added advantages, the procedure leading up to the real culmination, which is the hangover. It is the same in the game of Schlemiel: the mess-making, which attracts the most attention, is merely a pleasure-giving way for White to lead up to the crux, which is obtaining forgiveness from Black.

For the Alcoholic the hangover is not as much the physical pain as the psychological torment. The two favorite pastimes of drinking people are "Martini" (how many drinks and how they were mixed) and "Morning After" (let me tell you about my hangover). "Martini" is played, for the most part, by social drinkers; many alcoholics prefer a hard round of psychological "Morning After," and organizations such as A.A. offer him an unlimited opportunity for this.

Whenever one patient visited his psychiatrist after a binge, he would call himself all sorts of names; the psychiatrist said nothing. Later, recounting these visits in a therapy group, White said with smug satisfaction that it was the psychiatrist who had called him all those names. The main conversational interest of many alcoholics in the therapeutic situation is not their drinking, which they apparently mention mostly in deference to their persecutors, but their subsequent suffering. The transactional object of the drinking, aside from the personal pleasures it brings, is to set up a situation where the Child can be severely scolded not only by the internal Parent but by any parental figures in the environment who are interested enough to oblige. Hence the therapy of this game should be concentrated not on the drinking but on the morning after, the self-indulgence in self-castigation. There is a type of heavy drinker, however, who does not have hangovers, and such people do not belong in the present category.

There is also a game "Dry Alcoholic," in which White goes through the process of financial or social degradation without a bottle, making the same sequence of moves and requiring the same supporting cast. Here again, the morning after is the crux of the matter. Indeed, it is the similarity between "Dry Alcoholic" and regular "Alcoholic" which emphasizes that both are games; for example, the procedure for getting discharged from a job is the same in both. "Addict" is similar to "Alcoholic" but more sinister, more dramatic, more sensational and faster. In our society, at least, it leans more heavily on the readily available Persecutor, with Patsies and Rescuers being few and far between and the Connection playing a much more central role.

There are a variety of organizations involved in "Alcoholic," some of them national or even international in scope, others local. Many of them publish rules for the game. Nearly all of them explain how to play the role of Alcoholic: take a drink before breakfast, spend money allotted for other purposes, etc. They also explain the function of the Rescuer. Alcoholics Anonymous, for example, continues playing the actual game but concentrates on inducing the Alcoholic to take a role as Rescuer. Former Alcoholics are preferred because they know how the game goes, and hence are better qualified to play the supporting role than people who have never played before. Cases have been reported of a chapter of A.A. running out of Alcoholics to work on; whereupon the members resumed drinking, since there was no other way to continue the game in the absence of people to rescue.

There are also organizations devoted to improving the lot of the other players. Some put pressure on the spouses to shift their roles from Persecutor to Rescuer. The one which seems to come closest to the theoretical ideal of treatment deals with teen-age offspring of alcoholics; these young people are encouraged to break away from the game itself, rather than merely shift their roles.

The psychological cure of an alcoholic also lies in getting him to stop playing the game altogether, rather than simply change from one role to another. In some cases this has been feasible, although it is a difficult task to find something else as interesting to the Alcoholic as continuing his game. Since he is classically afraid of intimacy, the substitute may have to be another game rather than a game-free relationship. Often so-called cured alcoholics are not very stimulating company socially, and possibly they feel a lack of excitement in their lives and are continually tempted to go back to their old ways. The criterion of a true "game cure" is that the former Alcoholic should be able to drink socially without putting himself in jeopardy. The usual "total abstinence" cure will not satisfy the game analyst.

It is apparent from the description of this game that there is a strong temptation for the Rescuer to play "I'm Only Trying to Help You"; for the Persecutor to play "Look What You've Done to Me"; and for the Patsy* to play "Good Joe." With the rise of rescue organizations which publicize the idea that alcoholism is a disease, alcoholics have been taught to play "Wooden Leg." The law, which takes a special interest in such people, tends to encourage this nowadays. The emphasis has shifted from the Persecutor to the Rescuer, from "I am a sinner" to "What do you expect from a sick man?" (part of the trend in modern thinking away from religion and toward science). From an existential point of view it seems to have done little to diminish the sale of liquor to heavy drinkers. Nevertheless, Alcoholics Anonymous is still for most people the best initiation into the therapy of over-indulgence.

Antithesis

As is well known, "Alcoholic" is usually played hard and is difficult to give up. In one case a female alcoholic in a therapy group participated very little until she thought she knew enough about the other members to go ahead with her game. She then asked them to tell her what they thought of her. Since she had behaved pleasantly enough, various members said nice things about her, but she protests: "That's not what I want. I want to know what you really think." She made it clear that she was seeking derogatory comments. The other women refused to persecute her, whereupon she went home and told her husband that if she took another drink, he must either divorce her or send her to a hospital. He promised to do this, and that evening she became intoxicated and he sent her to a sanitarium. Here the other

---
*In underworld slang "patsy" once meant all right, or satisfactory, and later came to denote "pigeon."

100 AFFECTIVE PHASE

members refused to play the persecutory roles White assigned to them; she was unable to tolerate this antithetical behavior, in spite of everyone's behavior, in spite of everyone's efforts to reinforce whatever insight she had already obtained. At home she found someone who was willing to play the role she demanded.

In other cases, however, it appears possible to prepare the patient sufficiently so that the game can be given up, and to attempt a true social cure in which the therapist declines to play either Persecutor or Rescuer. It is equally untherapeutic for him to play the role of Patsy by allowing the patient to forego his financial and punctuality obligations. The correct therapeutic procedure from a transactional point of view is, after careful preliminary groundwork, to take an Adult contractual position and refuse to play any of the roles, hoping that the patient will be able to tolerate not only abstinence from drinking but also from playing his game. If he cannot, he is best referred to a Rescuer.

Antithesis is particularly difficult, because the heavy drinker is highly regarded in most Western countries as a desirable object for censure, concern or generosity, and someone who refuses to play any of these roles tends to arouse public indignation. A rational approach may be even more alarming to the Rescuers than to the Alcoholic, sometimes with unfortunate consequences to the therapy. In one clinical situation a group of workers were seriously interested in the game "Alcoholic" and were attempting to effect real cures by breaking up the game rather than merely rescuing the patients. As soon as this became apparent, they were frozen out by the lay committee which was backing the clinic, and none of them was ever again called on to assist in treating these patients.

Relatives

An interesting byplay in "Alcoholic" is called "Have One." This was discovered by a perceptive student of industrial psychiatry. White and his wife (a non-drinking Persecutor) go on a picnic with Black and his wife (both Patsies). White says to the Blacks, "Have One!" If they have one, this gives White license to have four or five. The game is unmasked if the Blacks refuse. White, by the rules of drinking, is then entitled to be insulted, and he will find more compliant companions for his next picnic. What appears at the social level to be Adult generosity, is at the psychological level an act of insolence, whereby White's Child obtains Parental indulgence from Black by open bribery under the very nose of Mrs. White, who is powerless to protest. Actually, it is just because she will be "powerless" to protest that Mrs. White consents to the whole arrangement, since she is just as axious for the game to continue, with herself in the role of Persecutor, as Mr. White is with himself in the role of Alcoholic. Her recriminations against him in the morning after the picnic are easy to image. This variant can cause complications in White is Black's boss.

In general the Patsy is not as badly off as the name implies. Patsies are often lonely people who have a great deal to gain by being nice to Alcoholics. The delicatessen man who plays "Good Joe" makes many acquaintances in this way, and he can get a good reputation in his own social circle not only as a generous person but also as a good storyteller.

One variant of "Good Joe," incidentally, is to go around asking for advice about how best to help people. This is an example of a jolly and constructive game worth encouraging. Its inverse is "Tough Guy" taking lessons in violence or asking for advice about how best to hurt people. Although the mayhem is never put into practice, the player has the privilege of associating with real tough guys who are playing for keeps, and can bask in their reflected glory. This is one species of what the French call *un fanfaron de vice*.

2. Participants complete the following questionnaire:

Eric Berne suggests that in order to meet basic psychological needs people assume roles and act out life games. Drinking is a game played for a variety of reasons. "Alcoholic" is a more serious lifelong game.

The following behaviors are likely to be associated with the drinking and alcoholic games. For each behavior, indicate likely participants and the reasons these players have for entering the game.
- a. Drinking to intoxication
- b. Exaggerating stories
- c. Risk taking (walking ledges, racing cars)
- d. Betraying confidences

3. The participants form groups of three to four members to discuss their responses on the questionnaire.
4. Instructor summarizes comments of the groups after asking the groups for their generalizations.

■ SOCIAL DRINKING SITUATIONS EXERCISE
☐ Purpose

Participants must understand that there are alternative behaviors in any alcohol-related situation. Disruptive behavior may occur if persons do not perceive that there are alternatives to any social drinking situation. Participants are encouraged in this activity to discover the alternatives available.

☐ Principles

Nonjudgmental, relevance, openness, risk taking

☐ Procedures

1. Participants individually respond to the following hypothetical situations:
   a. You're at a party. It's time to leave and your friend is driving. He's had too much to drink but so have you. What do you do?
   b. You're hosting a party and plan to serve beer. Four friends arrive in a car. Everyone has already been drinking, including the driver. They plan to drive home after your party. What do you do?
   c. You're in a bar with four friends, one of whom just bought the "first round." Standard procedure calls for a round from everyone before you leave. Your final exam in biology is the next day. What do you do?
   d. You're having a party with all your friends. After several hours of heavy drinking, the beer is gone. You've had as much as everyone, and are the only one with a car. You are elected to go out and get some more. What do you do?
   e. You're on your way home from a party. You are with a mixed group and everyone has done a lot of drinking. After repeated boasting about his athletic prowess, someone challenges Johnny Jock to climb a tree and swing into his open apartment window. Everyone encourages him to try. What do you do?
2. Participants form groups of three of four members to discuss each of their responses
3. A large group discussion follows with a review of all solutions.

■ DRINKING BEHAVIOR CONTINUUM

☐ Purpose

Instructor and participants may differ on values and feelings concerning alcohol-related behavior. Drinking behavior is personal. This activity allows persons to clarify their positions on alcohol drinking practices. In addition, participants have the opportunity to learn to appreciate and respect the positions of others.

☐ Principles

Nonjudgmental, relevance, openness, risk taking

☐ Procedures

1. Individuals complete the Drinking Behavior Continuum:

   Read each item and reflect individually on how you feel about that behavior right now. Then identify where that behavior would fit on your continuum and write the number for that behavior at that point on the line:

   |_____|_____|
   Acceptable   **Does not matter**   **Unacceptable**

   1. Never drinking an alcoholic beverage
   2. Drinking alcoholic beverages only with dinner
   3. Drinking wine with meals
   4. Drinking alcoholic beverages at lunch and dinner
   5. Drinking only on social occasions
   6. Drinking anytime one feels like it
   7. Having an "eye opener"
   8. Drinking to intoxication
   9. Drinking to intoxication frequently
   10. Drinking to intoxication whenever one feels like it
   11. Drinking alone
   12. Drinking alone to intoxication
   13. Giving an alcoholic beverage to a child
   14. Spiking the nonalcoholic beverage at a party
   15. Driving an automobile alone after drinking (feeling high)
   16. Driving an automobile alone while intoxicated
   17. Driving an automobile under the influence of alcohol with a friend in a car
   18. Driving an automobile under the influence of alcohol with your family in the car
   19. Riding in a car with a driver who has been drinking
   20. Letting a drunken friend drive home alone from a party
   21. Continuing to supply drinks to a drunken friend

2. Participants form groups of three to four members to discuss their responses to the continuum.
3. Group summarizes in one sentence what they felt they learned from completing the continuum.
4. Instructor summarizes that drinking behavior is personal and nonjudgmental.

■ IDEAL VS. REAL DRINKING BEHAVIOR
☐ **Purpose**

Discrepancies exist between what individuals consider to be their actual drinking behavior and their ideal drinking behavior. Participants should be aware that in order to live consistently with personal values their real and ideal behavior should be closely aligned. This exercise creates discomfort for those who find clear inconsistencies in their behavior. The stress encountered in this activity may be alleviated by a commitment to positive drinking practices.

☐ **Principles**

Nonjudgmental, relevance, openness, risk taking

☐ **Procedures**

1. Participants refer to the Drinking Behavior Continuum Exercise and complete the continuum.
2. Participants circle the number on the left-hand margin corresponding to the activities in which they have engaged.
3. Participants star the number corresponding to the activities that were unacceptable to them.
4. Each participant counts the number of activities that have both a circle and a star.
5. Participants form groups of three to four members and total items with both a circle and a star.
6. Instructor records group totals on the chalkboard.
7. Instructor comments on inconsistency of the behavior and does not accept participant rationalization.

■ ALCOHOL COMMITMENT ACTIVITY
☐ **Purpose**

The goal of affective alcohol education culminates in this activity. Participants have the opportunity to commit themselves to positive alcohol-related behavior. The actualization of the commitment follows immediately in behavior transferred outside of the instructional situation.

☐ **Principles**

Nonjudgmental, relevance, openness, risk taking, and commitment/actualization

☐ **Procedure**

Participants are asked to make a commitment concerning their drinking behavior.

■ AFFECTIVE EVALUATION ACTIVITY

Affective activities are not evaluated in the traditional sense of academic assessment. The goals of affective activity, integration of cognitions and values into actual behavior, are inconsistent with assigning letter grades to people. The valuing process cannot be reduced to a point system.

The facilitator, however, needs feedback regarding the degree to which the principles of affective activity—nonjudgmental, relevance, openness, risk taking, commitment/actualization—are being realized in this instructional situation. At different points in the instructional process the facilitator can make use of affective questionnaires. If the questionnaires yields positive results, the facilitator proceeds. But if the participants feel the facilitator is "not concerned," "very closed," or the activities are "worthless" or "of no importance," group discussions are used to isolate the problem and generate alternate actions. The problem must be identified and solved before cognitions can be integrated with affective reaction to change behavior.

AFFECTIVE QUESTIONNAIRE I

This form was designed to evaluate the affective activities that you have experienced. Please answer as honestly as you can the following questions in regard to what you experienced during the group discussion activities. This is an anonymous form and it will not be used for student evaluation.

DIRECTIONS: Place a check beside the response that best describes *your feelings* about the affective activities you have experienced.

1. As a result of these experiences, *I* feel that the instructor.
   - ☐ Fully accepted our feelings
   - ☐ Partially accepted our feelings
   - ☐ Grudgingly accepted our feelings
   - ☐ Rejected our feelings
2. As a result of these experiences, *I* feel the instructor demonstrated
   - ☐ Much concern for my feelings
   - ☐ Some concern for my feelings
   - ☐ Little concern for my feelings
   - ☐ No concern for my feelings
3. Responsible drinking behavior is
   - ☐ Very important
   - ☐ Important
   - ☐ Not very important
   - ☐ Of no importance
4. In the affective activity I participated in *I* felt that I was
   - ☐ Very open
   - ☐ Moderately open
   - ☐ Moderately closed
   - ☐ Very closed

AFFECTIVE QUESTIONNAIRE I–cont'd

5. In the affective activity I experienced *I* felt the instructor was
   - ☐ Very open
   - ☐ Moderately open
   - ☐ Moderately closed
   - ☐ Very closed
6. In my interaction with the instructor I would say that *I* am
   - ☐ Very open
   - ☐ Moderately open
   - ☐ Moderately closed
   - ☐ Very closed
7. In the affective activity I participated in *I* felt that the group in which I participated was
   - ☐ Very open
   - ☐ Moderately open
   - ☐ Moderately closed
   - ☐ Very closed
8. As a result of the affective instruction *I* felt susceptible to the alcohol problems
   - ☐ Very much
   - ☐ Moderately
   - ☐ Not much
   - ☐ Not at all
9. In the affective activity I experienced *I* felt as if I was taking a
   - ☐ High risk
   - ☐ Moderate risk
   - ☐ Low risk
   - ☐ No risk
10. In the affective activity I experienced *I* felt as if I was taking a
    - ☐ High risk
    - ☐ Moderate risk
    - ☐ Low risk
    - ☐ No risk
11. As a result of my risk taking in the affective activity *I* feel
    - ☐ Very good
    - ☐ Moderately good
    - ☐ Moderately disturbed
    - ☐ Very disturbed
12. Risk taking is something *I* would like to
    - ☐ Continue
    - ☐ Work on
    - ☐ Forget

AFFECTIVE QUESTIONNAIRE II

This form was designed to evaluate the affective activities that you have experienced. Please answer as honestly as you can the following questions in regard to what you experienced during the group discussion activities. This is an anonymous form and it will not be used for student evaluation.

DIRECTIONS: Place a check beside the response that best describes *your feelings* about the affective activities you have experienced.

1. In the affective activity I experienced I felt as if *I* were
   - ☐ Fully leveling
   - ☐ Partially leveling
   - ☐ Slightly leveling
   - ☐ Not leveling
2. In the affective activity I experienced I felt as if *others* were
   - ☐ Fully leveling
   - ☐ Partially leveling
   - ☐ Slightly leveling
   - ☐ Not leveling
3. In my interaction with the instructor I would say that *I* was
   - ☐ Fully leaving
   - ☐ Partially leveling
   - ☐ Slightly leveling
   - ☐ Not leveling
4. As a result of the affective activity I experienced *I* feel as though the *instructor* was
   - ☐ Fully leveling
   - ☐ Partially leveling
   - ☐ Slightly leveling
   - ☐ Not leveling
5. As a result of these affective activities I feel as if *I* am
   - ☐ Fully open
   - ☐ Moderately open
   - ☐ Moderately closed
   - ☐ Fully closed
6. As a result of these affective activities I feel as if *I* am
   - ☐ Fully leveling
   - ☐ Partially leveling
   - ☐ Slightly leveling
   - ☐ Not leveling
7. As a result of these affective activities I feel as if *I* am taking a
   - ☐ High risk
   - ☐ Moderate risk
   - ☐ Slight risk
   - ☐ No risk

AFFECTIVE QUESTIONNAIRE II–cont'd

8. Responsible drinking behavior is
   - ☐ Very important
   - ☐ Important
   - ☐ Not very important
   - ☐ Of no importance
9. How confident are you that you can live by your commitment?
   - ☐ Very confident
   - ☐ Moderately confident
   - ☐ Slightly confident
   - ☐ Not confident
10. As a result of affective activities *I* learned
    - ☐ Much about myself
    - ☐ Something about myself
    - ☐ Little about myself
    - ☐ Nothing about myself
11. As a result of affective activities *I* learned
    - ☐ Much about others
    - ☐ Something about others
    - ☐ Little about others
    - ☐ Nothing about others
12. Having experienced affective activities *I* feel the activities were
    - ☐ Very beneficial in teaching
    - ☐ Moderately beneficial in teaching
    - ☐ Slightly beneficial in teaching
    - ☐ Of no benefit in teaching

■ SUMMARY

Affective alcohol activities are designed to facilitate alcohol decision making. By expressing feelings related to alcohol use and values clarification the learners examine personal drinking behavior. Facilitators use the suggested activities at appropriate times in the instructional procedure. Activities range in involvement from casual introductions to intimate value sharing.

■ REFERENCES

1. Shuell, T. J., and Lee, C. Z.: Learning and instruction, Belmont, Calif., 1976, Wadsworth Publishing Co., p. 179.
2. Engs, R. C., Barnes, E. S., and Wantz, M.: Health games students play, Dubuque, Iowa, 1975, Kendall/Hunt Publishing Co.
3. Livingston, S. A.: Simulation games and attitude change: attitudes towards the poor, report no. 63, Baltimore, April, 1970, Center for the Study of Social Organizations of Schools, John Hopkins University.
4. DeKock, P.: Simulations and changes in racial attitudes, Soc. Educ., Feb., 1969, pp. 181-183.

APPENDIXES

A ALCOHOL BEHAVIOR INVENTORY*

The Alcohol Behavior Inventory (ABI) is a two-part questionnaire. Part one of the questionnaire involves demographic data. Part two deals with the amount and frequency of consumer drinking and consumer alcohol-related behavior. The ABI also focuses primarily on measures of disruptive behavior. The ABI is administered and completed anonymously.

The ABI provides activated health education with two important features, external evaluation and instructor accountability. The stated goal of the Alcohol Instruction Model is to instill responsible alcohol-related behavior in the students. The inventory, given in a pretest-posttest fashion with control groups allows for objective measurement of the effects of activated alcohol education.

---

*This inventory was developed from funds provided in part by Eastern Area Alcohol Education and Training Program, Inc., Hartford, Conn., 1976-1977 (contract no. 50-1932A-B).

ALCOHOL BEHAVIOR INVENTORY

This is an anonymous questionnaire. Part one involves information concerning your present situation. Part two deals with the amount and frequency of your drinking behavior during a 7-day period. In this questionnaire there are no right or wrong answers. Please be truthful and take your time in order to ensure accurate answers. Please do not discuss the questions with anyone.

To facilitate the final analysis of data, a coding system will be used. Please write a name, *not your own,* in the space provided that you will be able to recall in one month.

Code name_____

PART ONE

DIRECTIONS:: *Mark only one answer to each item.* If you have a question, raise your hand and the instructor will attend to you at your seat.

1. How old are you in years? __16__
2. Circle which sex you are: __Female__   Male
3. a. Do you live with your parents? (Circle one.) (Yes) No
   b. If you *do not* live with your parents, circle the number that best describes where you do live:

ALCOHOL BEHAVIOR INVENTORY—cont'd

   (1) Dormitory
   (2) Private house
   (3) Other _____
4. In an average week, about how much money, in dollars, do you have available to spend as you wish on nonessentials? (Going out, recreation, etc.)
   a. $5 and under
   b. $6-$15
   c. $16-$20
   d. $31-$45
   e. $46 and above
5. Circle your race/ethnicity:
   a. White
   b. Black
   c. Oriental or Asian American
   d. American Indian
   e. Spanish American (Mexican, Puerto Rican, Latin American.)
   f. Other _____
6. Circle your religion:
   a. Catholic
   b. Protestant
   c. Jewish
   d. None
   e. Other _____
7. Circle the number of times you have attended religious services during the last month:
   a. None
   b. One
   c. Two
   d. Three
   e. Four
   f. Five or more

PART TWO

DIRECTIONS: Describe your drinking behavior in the last week. Confine your answers to the previous 7-day period. For the purposes of this survey a drink will be defined as equal to one cocktail, one glass of beer, one glass of wine, or one short of liquor. The definition for "under the influence of alcohol" should be interpreted as being in a state of feeling high, being dizzy, feeling sick, being impaired, or having an interruption of the normal routine.

8. During the last 7 days, on how many *days* did you drink alcoholic beverages? _____ (If your answer is *none*, please move to questions 23, 24 and 25.)
9. For each of those days on which you drank, estimate the *number of drinks* that you had:
   Monday _____   Thursday _____   Sunday _____
   Tuesday _____   Friday _____   Monday _____
   Wednesday _____   Saturday _____
10. Circle the number of times during the previous 7-day period you perceived yourself to be under the influence of alcohol:
    a. None
    b. One time
    c. Two times
    d. Three times
    e. Four or more times

Continued.

ALCOHOL BEHAVIOR INVENTORY—cont'd

11. Circle the type of drink you usually had on those occasions:
    a. Beer
    b. Liquor (gin, rum, whiskey, cocktail, etc.)
    c. Wine
    d. Combination
12. Circle with whom you drank *most often* during the previous 7 days:
    a. Immediate family
    b. Other relatives
    c. Friends and acquaintances
    d. Alone
13. Circle the number of times during the previous seven 7-day period you have been involved in a *serious argument* while or after you have been drinking:
    a. None
    b. One time
    c. Two times
    d. Three times
    e. Four or more times
14. Circle the number of times during the previous 7-day period you have been involved in *physical fights* while or after you have been drinking:
    a. None
    b. One time
    c. Two times
    d. Three times
    e. Four or more times
15. Circle the number of times during the previous 7-day period you have been involved in the *destruction of property* while or after you have been drinking:
    a. None
    b. One time
    c. Two times
    d. Three times
    e. Four or more times
16. Circle the number of times during the previous 7-day period you have been *involved in dangerous behavior* (for example, ride on outside of cars, set off fire alarms, walk on high ledges, etc.) during or after drinking:
    a. None
    b. One time
    c. Two times
    d. Three times
    e. Four or more times
17. Circle the number of times during the previous 7-day period you have *encouraged someone else to engage in dangerous behavior* (for example, ride on outside of cars, set off fire alarms, walk on high ledges, etc.) during or after drinking:
    a. None
    b. One time
    c. Two times
    d. Three times
    e. Four or more times
18. Circle the number of times during the previous 7-day period you have gotten into *trouble* with the police or school authorities during or after drinking:
    a. None
    b. One time
    c. Two times
    d. Three times
    e. Four or more times
19. Circle the number of times during the previous 7-day period you have been *involved in stealing or shoplifting* during or after drinking:
    a. None
    b. One time
    c. Two times
    d. Three times
    e. Four or more times

ALCOHOL BEHAVIOR INVENTORY—cont'd

20. Circle the number of *times* during the previous 7-day period you have *ridden* in an automobile with a driver who was under the influence of alcohol (feeling high, feeling sick, dizzy, etc.):
    a. None
    b. One time
    c. Two times
    d. Three times
    e. Four or more times

21. Circle the number of *miles* you have *ridden* in an automobile in which you perceived the driver to be under the influence of alcohol (feeling high, feeling sick, dizzy, etc.) during the previous 7-day period:
    a. None
    b. One to five miles
    c. Six to twenty-five miles
    d. Twenty-six to seventy-four miles
    e. Seventy-five or more miles

22. Circle the number of *times* during the previous 7-day period you have *driven* an automobile while you perceived yourself to be under the influence of alcohol:
    a. None
    b. One time
    c. Two times
    d. Three times
    e. Four or more times

23. Circle the number of *miles* you have *driven* an automobile while you perceived yourself to be under the influence of alcohol (feeling high, feeling sick, dizzy, etc.) during the previous 7-day period:
    a. None
    b. One to five miles
    c. Six to twenty-five miles
    d. Twenty-six to seventy-four miles
    e. Seventy-five or more miles

24. Circle the number of times during the previous 7-day period you have been in an *automobile traveling over 70 mph* while or after the driver had been drinking:
    a. None
    b. One time
    c. Two times
    d. Three times
    e. Four or more times

25. Circle the number of times during the previous 7-day period you have been in an *automobile accident/traffic violation* while or after the driver (you or someone else) had been drinking:
    a. None
    b. One time
    c. Two times
    d. Three times
    e. Four or more times

■ RELIABILITY OF THE ABI

The reliability of the ABI was assessed by a test-retest method. The inventory was administered three times to the twenty-four students. A one-month interval separated the three administrations of the ABI.

A Pearson product-moment correlation coefficient *(r)* was used to estimate the test-retest reliability of the three dependent variables (drinking severity, non-automobile-related disruptive behavior, and automobile-related disruptive behavior) in the inventory. The correlation between the pretest and each posttest for each of the three variables was computed.

Table A-1. A Pearson product-moment correlation for the three dependent variables between the pretest and the two posttests

Variables	Pretest with posttest (1)	Pretest with posttest (2)
Drinking severity	0.701	0.777
Non-automobile-related disruptive behavior	0.872	0.490
Automobile-related disruptive behavior	0.613	0.603

The findings, as reported in Table A-1, show that the test-retest reliability is high and that the ABI is a reliable instrument for measuring the self-reported drinking behavior of university students.

■ VALIDITY OF THE ABI

The content validity of the ABI was established by studying the items on the ABI to see if they appeared to be suitable measures of alcohol-related behavior. Two specialists in the area of instrument development, one from the Educational Psychology Department at the State University College at Fredonia and the other from the Department of Social and Preventive Medicine at SUNYAB, were asked to examine each item on the ABI and judge whether each was measuring either drinking severity or alcohol-related disruptive behavior. Both experts agreed that the sixteen items on the ABI appeared to be measuring alcohol-related behavior; therefore the ABI was considered to have content validity.

In order to examine the construct validity of the ABI the inventory was administered to two groups of university students assumed to be at the opposite ends of the drinking continuum. The one group consisted of those university students belonging to the Crusade for Christ movement, a religious group on campus that encourages an alcohol abstinence policy. It was assumed that students with this religious affiliation would score low for alcohol-related behavior when administered the ABI. The other group consisted of students found in a local drinking establishment during the early morning hours on a given week night. It was assumed that these university students were frequent and heavy student drinkers and that they would score high on the ABI.

In order to obtain data on the alcohol-related drinking behavior of students in an abstinence setting, the ABI was administered to the college students during a meeting of the Crusade for Christ movement. Students affiliated with this campus movement taking part in a bible study session conducted at Norton Hall on the SUNYAB Campus were asked to take part in the alcohol research project and fill out an ABI. A brief account of the purpose of the study was presented to this sample population before administration of the ABI. The procedure used for the administration of the inventory was the same as the procedure used on other sampling occasions.

Table A-2. The *t*-test for difference between means for drinking severity

Group	Mean scores	Variance	Standard deviation	Test statistic
Abstinence (n = 74)	1.175	0.3660	0.6050	14.504*
Drinking (n = 25)	26.280	225.1267	15.0042	

*P < 0.01.

Table A-3. The *t*-test for difference between means for non-automobile-related disruptive behavior

Group	Mean scores	Variance	Standard deviation	Test statistic
Abstinence (n = 74)	7.000	0.0000	0.0000	7.616*
Drinking (n = 25)	7.800	0.8333	0.9129	

*P < 0.01.

Table A-4. The *t*-test for difference between means for automobile-related disruptive behavior

Group	Mean scores	Variance	Standard deviation	Test statistic
Abstinence (n = 74)	6.1622	0.5213	0.7220	7.085*
Drinking (n = 25)	9.0400	10.8733	3.2975	

*P < 0.01.

In acquiring a population sample of frequent heavy drinkers, the students found at the Wilkenson Pub on the SUNYAB campus after 1:00 AM on a given weekend night were solicited to take part in the alcohol research project. All students found drinking in this establishment at this early morning hour were asked to come to the Department of Health Education the following Tuesday to fill out the ABI. The purpose of the study was briefly explained and appointment cards given to each student who volunteered to participate. The students were informed that they would be reimbursed two dollars for their cooperation in the study. On that following Tuesday the procedure used for administering the ABI to these students was the same as on other sampling occasions.

The scores for drinking severity, non-automobile-related and automobile-related disruptive behavior were compared between both groups. A *t*-test for the difference between two independent means was calculated for each of the three variables.

The data presented in Table A-2 shows the difference in the means for drinking severity between the two study populations. The rejection region with ninety-seven degrees of freedom was calculated to be ≥ 2.35. With the observed test statistic of 14.504 being greater than the rejection region, the difference in the two populations was found significant at the 0.01 level.

When the mean scores for non-automobile-related disruptive behavior were compared, a statistically significiant difference between the two groups was found. The observed test statistic was 7.62 (Table A-3). This value was ≥ 2.35; therefore the populations were found statistically different at the 0.01 level.

The observed value of the test statistic for the difference between the mean scores for automobile-related disruptive behavior, as illustrated in Table A-4, was also found significant at the 0.01 level.

B REVIEW TESTS (COGNITIVE INFORMATION)

Review tests were developed for use as one component in the internal feedback system. Alternate form testing can be employed to evaluate the retention of information disseminated during the cognitive phase. This form of testing accomplished three objectives:

1. The consumers had the advantage of receiving immediate feedback on their strengths and weaknesses, providing a learning experience for them.
2. Consumers have an increased opportunity for success and positive reinforcement in their efforts at mastering the material.
3. The proper emphasis on learning is maximized by reducing anxieties regarding grading.

■ REVIEW

Name _____ Section _____

Multiple choice

_____ 1. When an individual begins to have difficulty in relating to others and his drinking becomes repetitive, he is considered in what stage of health?
   a. Optimal
   b. Incipient illness
   c. Overt illness
   d. Critical illness

_____ 2. An individual is considered legally driving while intoxicated if the BAC level is:
   a. 0.02-0.03
   b. 0.07-0.10
   c. 0.30-0.40
   d. 0.50-0.60

_____ 3. In all states a person is considered driving while intoxicated if the BAC level is at or above which of the following levels:
   a. 0.07
   b. 0.10
   c. 0.15
   d. 0.60

_____ 4. A person is considered suffering from alcoholism when he is in what stage of health:
   a. Optimal health
   b. Incipient illness
   c. Overt illness
   d. None of these

118 APPENDIXES

___ 5. The cause(s) of alcoholism is:
    a. Physiological
    b. Psychosocial
    c. Both a and b
    d. None of these

___ 6. Which does *not* affect absorption?
    a. Concentration of alcohol
    b. Amount of food in the stomach
    c. Amount of nonalcoholic substances in alcoholic beverages
    d. Body weight

___ 7. The average rate of oxidation of alcohol per hour is:
    a. 9.9 ml (1/3 oz)
    b. 22.5 ml (3/4 oz)
    c. 60 ml (2 oz)
    d. 120 ml (4 oz)

___ 8. The rate of sobering can be accelerated by:
    a. Drinking black coffee
    b. Taking cold showers
    c. Exercising
    d. Exposure to fresh air
    e. None of these

___ 9. The condition in which increasingly larger amounts of alcohol are required to produce the effect formerly obtained by smaller doses is called:
    a. Physiological tolerance
    b. Habituation
    c. Physiological dependence
    d. Psychological dependence

___ 10. A large accumulation of acetaldehyde in the body will produce the physiological effect commonly known as:
    a. Withdrawal
    b. Hangover
    c. Blackout
    d. Tolerance

ANSWERS: 1. b, 2. b, 3. c, 4. c, 5. c, 6. d, 7. a, 8. e, 9. a, 10. b.

☐ **Alternate Review 1**

DIRECTIONS: Please place the word *true* (T) or *false* (F) in the space provided.

___ 1. When an individual exhibits normative behavior, he may be said to be in the incipient illness stage.

___ 2. Blood alcohol concentration is the ratio of alcohol present in the blood to the total volume of blood.

___ 3. In New York State one is considered legally driving while intoxicated if the blood alcohol level is 0.10.

___ 4. The etiology of alcoholism is primarily physiological.

___ 5. The by-products of alcohol oxidation are eliminated from the body as water and carbon dioxide.

___ 6. A small fraction of alcohol is eliminated unchanged, through the lungs or in perspiration and urine.

___ 7. Like other foods, alcohol requires digestion.

___ 8. The greater the concentration of alcohol in a beverage, the more rapid will be the rate of absorption.

___ 9. Large quantities of alchol may irritate the lining of the stomach, often resulting in long-lasting inflammation called gastritis.
___ 10. The psychological factor is not thought to play a major part in the case of the experienced drinker's tolerance to alcohol.

ANSWERS: 1. F, 2. T, 3. T, 4. F, 5. T, 6. T, 7. F, 8. T, 9. T, 10. F.

■ REVIEW

Name _____ Section _____

Multiple choice

___ 1. Moskowitz's study attempted to test the relationship of alcohol to:
   a. Memory
   b. Decision making
   c. Information processing
   d. The brain

___ 2. Verhaehen's study found that at BACs of 50 mg/ml and 60 mg/ml information processing slowed:
   a. At a statistically significant level
   b. At a statistically insignificant level
   c. For the older subjects only
   d. For the younger subjects only

___ 3. Moskowitz proved that response latency significantly increases with:
   a. The number of possible alternative responses
   b. The amount of alcohol
   c. Neither a or b
   d. Both a and b

___ 4. An empirical study is one in which:
   a. Case and control groups are used
   b. Validated scientific instrument(s) is used
   c. Random selection of subjects is used
   d. Experimental statistical analysis is used
   e. All of the above

___ 5. In Boyatzis's study on aggression:
   a. Individuals who consumed nonalcoholic beverages were more agressive than those who drank alcoholic beverages
   b. Distilled spirits drinkers were more aggressive than beer drinkers
   c. There was no significant difference between the control group, distilled spirits group, and the beer drinking group
   d. The collegiate drinking group had to be eliminated from the study because of their overaggressive tendencies

120 APPENDIXES

____ 6. In Hetherington's study on aggression:
   a. It was concluded that alcohol seemed to facilitate the expression of repressed aggressive needs in humor
   b. The humor preference of subjects was investigated
   c. High aggression subjects rated aggressive cartoons as funnier than did low aggressive subjects
   d. All of the above

____ 7. The search for relaxation has led an increasing number of people to:
   a. Biofeedback
   b. Meditation
   c. Exercise
   d. Use of alcohol and other depressant drugs
   e. All of the above

____ 8. In the study on alcohol and relaxation by Girdano and Yarian the means used to determine the state of relaxation was:
   a. Questionnaires
   b. Electromyographic equipment
   c. Verbal response
   d. Alpha waves

____ 9. In the study on alcohol and relaxation the muscle tension of the experimental group after alcohol ingestion:
   a. Increased
   b. Decreased
   c. Remained the same
   d. Fluctuated depending on amounts consumed
   e. None of the above

____ 10. A double blind study is one in which:
   a. The subjects have lost sight in both eyes
   b. Blindfolds are used
   c. Both subjects and experimenters never learn the results
   d. Both subjects and experimenters are not aware of the subject membership in either the case or control group.
   e. None of the above

ANSWERS: 1. c, 2. a, 3. d, 4. e, 5. b, 6. d, 7. e, 8. b, 9. c, 10. d.

☐ **Alternate Review 2**

DIRECTIONS: Please place the word *true* (T) or *false* (F) in the space provided.

____ 1. In the study on alcohol and relaxation by Girdano and Yarian, a biofeedback technique was used to determine the degree of relaxation.

____ 2. In the study by Girdano and Yarian, muscle tension decreased 1 hour after the ingestion of alcohol.

APPENDIXES **121**

___ 3. A control group is not always needed in conducting an empirical valid study.
___ 4. Moskowitz demonstrated that response latency decreases as the alternatives increase.
___ 5. Statistical significance is commonly set at the .05 level.
___ 6. Boyatzis's study found that party attendance increases aggression.
___ 7. Medical students in Boyd's study increased test response time with 45 ml of alcohol.
___ 8. Mediation, alcohol, and biofeedback are methods used by some to relax.
___ 9. Hetherington investigated mood changes in college students.
___ 10. Moskowitz provided evidence that alcohol slows performance of tasks involving central processing of information.

ANSWERS: 1. T, 2. F, 3. F, 4. F, 5. T, 6. F, 7. T, 8. T, 9. F, 10. T.

■ REVIEW

Name _____ Section _____

Multiple choice

___ 1. The results of Evan's study on blood alcohol concentration and psychomotor performance demonstrated that:
   a. Alcohol produced a linear relationship between BAC and impairment in performance on most of the tests
   b. At a BAC of 0.08 all subjects revealed impairment for most of the tests
   c. Increasing BAC levels resulted in a significant decrease in stability of stance
   d. Mental performance decreased with increasing BAC levels
   e. All the above

___ 2. In Cohen's study on risk taking the conclusion drawn showed that in relation to their driving performance the drivers under the influence of alcohol tended to:
   a. Overrate their ability
   b. Underrate their ability
   c. Remain unchanged
   d. None of the above

___ 3. In Idestrom's study on the effects of alcohol, which of the following item(s) was tested:
   a. Choice-reaction time
   b. Bimanual hand coordination
   c. Standing steadiness
   d. All of the above
   e. None of the above

___ 4. Sideu found that on the eye-hand coordination test subjects who had ingested alcohol:
   a. Performed better than the controls
   b. Experienced their greatest decrement in performance
   c. Experienced their least decrement in performance
   d. Sideu did not test for eye-hand coordination

5. Idestrom's study revealed that the performance of subjects who drank alcohol was worst:
   a. Immediately after ingestion
   b. 15-30 minutes after ingestion
   c. 30-60 minutes after ingestion
   d. Over 1 hour after ingestion
6. In Idestrom's study, in the alcohol group, impairment of coordination was affected at:
   a. Low levels of alcohol
   b. High levels of alcohol only
   c. The same BAC as standing steadiness
   d. The same BAC as Bourdon's test
7. In Cohen's study, as the drivers consumed more alcohol:
   a. Their estimation of success in the driving task deteriorated
   b. Their actual success in the driving task deteriorated
   c. Neither a nor b
   d. Both a and b
8. Moskowitz and DePry determined that alcohol significantly affects:
   a. Vigilance tasks
   b. Coordination tasks
   c. Simple reaction time
   d. Divided attention tasks
9. Boyd's experiment with students showed that at 0.045 BAC reaction time slowed:
   a. 0%   c. 14%
   b. 5%   d. 25%
10. Huntley found that reaction time was seriously impaired after:
    a. One drink   c. Five drinks
    b. Three drinks   d. Ten drinks

ANSWERS: 1. e, 2. a, 3. d, 4. b, 5. c, 6. a, 7. d, 8. d, 9. c, 10. b.

☐ **Alternate Review 3**

DIRECTIONS: Please place the word *true* (T) or *false* (F) in the space provided.

1. In Evan's study on the effects of blood alcohol concentrations on psychomotor performance, the results demonstrated that alcohol produced a linear relationship between BAC and impairment in performance.
2. In Evan's study all subjects in the experimental group revealed impairment on most of the test when the blood alcohol level was 0.08.
3. In Cohen's study on risk taking, professional bus drivers were used.
4. From the results of Cohen's study the author concluded that alcohol intensified a driver's tendency to overrate his driving ability in relation to his actual driving performance.

_____ 5. In Cohen's study, as the drivers consumed more alcohol, they were prepared to drive through narrower gaps.
_____ 6. The purpose of Idestrom's study was to examine large doses of alcohol on psychomotor performance.
_____ 7. In Idestrom's study, impaired performance was obtained in all psychomotor and perceptual tests.
_____ 8. Sideu's study revealed the greatest decrement in performance in the alcohol group.
_____ 9. Moskowitz and DePry found conclusively that alcohol affected tone detection vigilance task.
_____ 10. Boyd's study resulted in net increase in response time of about 14% after ingestion of 45 ml of alcohol.

ANSWERS: 1. T, 2. T, 3. T, 4. T, 5. T, 6. F, 7. T, 8. T, 9. F, 10. T.

■ REVIEW

Name _____ Section _____

Multiple choice

_____ 1. In Bjerver and Goldberg's study on the effects of alcohol ingestion on driving ability:
   a. The subjects were divided into a beer group and a distilled spirits group
   b. The subjects were divided at random into control and alcohol groups
   c. The subjects were given a driving test
   d. The subjects were given a laboratory test
   e. All of the above

_____ 2. The result of the Bjerver and Goldberg study showed:
   a. The control group's driving remained the same
   b. The ingestion of alcohol decreased the time needed to perform the driving test
   c. The presence of alcohol in the blood deteriorated the capacity to drive a car by 25% to 30%
   d. All of the above

_____ 3. The laboratory test in the Bjerver and Goldberg study consisted of:
   a. A flicker test
   b. A blink test
   c. A standing steadiness test
   d. a and b
   e. a and c

_____ 4. The road test in the Bjerver and Goldberg study consisted of:
   a. A garage test
   b. Steering test
   c. Turning test
   d. Only a and b
   e. a, b, and c

124 APPENDIXES

___ 5. The case group in Haddon's study on pedestrian fatalities was tested for blood alcohol levels by:
   a. A breath test
   b. A sweat test
   c. Urine analysis
   d. Autopsy blood tests
   e. None of the above

___ 6. In comparing the case group with the control group in the Haddon study the following results were found:
   a. 67% of the control group had a blood alcohol level of zero
   b. 26% of the case group had a blood alcohol level of zero
   c. Blood alcohol levels of the control group were close to 40% higher than the case group
   d. a and b
   e. None of the above

___ 7. The size of the control group in Haddon's study as compared to the case group was:
   a. Larger
   b. Smaller
   c. Exactly the same
   d. Not controlled for in the study

___ 8. In McCarrol's study on fatal automobile accidents the control group was matched with the case group on the following characteristic(s):
   a. Sex
   b. Accident site
   c. Time of day
   d. Day of the week
   e. All of the above

___ 9. In the McCarrol study, when comparing the case with the control group, the large control group was found not to have a single driver with a blood alcohol level above:
   a. 50 mg/100 ml
   b. 100 mg/100 ml
   c. 150 mg/100 ml
   d. 200 mg/100 ml
   e. 250 mg/100 ml

___ 10. In the McCarrol study the results showed:
   a. Among drivers rated as probably responsible for their accidents, 73% had been drinking
   b. The greatest difference between the case and control group was in the age of the driver
   c. Women are terrible drivers
   d. The control group was similar to the case group in blood alcohol levels
   e. None of the above

ANSWERS: 1. e, 2. c, 3. d, 4. e, 5. d, 6. d, 7. a, 8. e, 9. e, 10. a.

☐ **Alternate Review 4**

DIRECTIONS: Please place the word *true* (T) or *false* (F) in the space provided.

___ 1. In Goldberg's study on the effects of alcohol on driving ability, the subjects in the control group improved their driving results.

___ 2. In Goldberg's study the ingestion of alcohol was positively correlated wtih an increase in driving performance time.
___ 3. In Goldberg's study at blood alcohol levels of 0.04 and 0.05, the capacity to drive a car deteriorated by 25% to 30%.
___ 4. The purpose of the McCarroll and Haddon study on automobile fatalities was to compare those fatally injured with accident groups at the same location.
___ 5. The comparison group was matched with the case group in McCarroll's study on the basis of sex, exact accident site, time of day, and day of the week.
___ 6. In Haddon's study, of the 50 pedestrians fatally injured, those who had been drinking outnumbered those who had not by about a 3 to 1 margin.
___ 7. In Haddon's study with pedestrians, the cases were not significantly more alcohol influenced than with age- and sex-matched members of the control group.
___ 8. In McCarroll's study, drinking drivers who were responsible for their accidents outnumbered noninvolved drinking drivers by about 3 to 1.
___ 9. In McCarroll's study, only about 10% of the control group drivers had a blood alcohol level of 0.25 or higher.
___ 10. The presence of alcohol in the blood at the 0.01 to 0.04 levels proved to be significantly more risky to the pedestrian in Haddon's study.

ANSWERS: 1. T, 2. T, 3. T, 4. F, 5. T, 6. T, 7. F, 8. T, 9. F, 10. T.

INDEX

A

Absorption of alcohol, 41-43
Abstainers, 11-12, 18-19
Acceptance of feelings in affective instruction, 81-82
Accidents; *see* Automobile accidents; Drivers, drinking; Pedestrian accidents; Home accidents
Acetaldehyde in alcohol oxidation, 48
Acetic acid in alcohol oxidation, 48-49
Activated health education, 2-10
  evaluation of, 8-9
  instructional model for, 3-8
  intervention strategy in, 8
  research related to, 9-10
  theory and principles of, 3-8
Actualization of new behaviors in affective instruction, 82-83
Adolescents
  as abstainers, 18
  alienation and drinking in, 88
  delinquent, 21-22
  drinking practices of, 13-15, 21-22
  and sex differences in, 14
Affective evaluation activity, 103-107
Affective method of instruction, 81-83
Affective phase of activated health education, 75-107
Age in alcohol-related automobile accidents, 23
Aggression, 58-59
  alcohol-related, 23-25
    in college students, 22
    theories of, 24-25
  effects of alcohol on, 21
  increase in, with alcohol, 90-91
Aggressive fantasies during drinking, 24
Alcohol
  absorption of, 41-43
  abuse of
    and health status continuum, 34-37
    programs related to, observation of, 4-5
  concentration and absorption of, 41
  effects of, on specific organs or functions, 49-54
  fetal syndrome of, 54
  and illicit drugs, 13-14

Alcohol—cont'd
  pharmacological properties of, 39-40
  physiological effects of, 6
  quantity ingested and absorption, 41
Alcohol Behavior Inventory, 9, 110-116
Alcohol commitment activity, 103
Alcohol concern exercise (activity), 95-96
Alcohol education, behavioral studies of, 9-10
Alcohol education relevancy exercise (activity), 95
Alcohol hepatitis, 50
Alcoholic beverages, processing of, 40-41
Alcoholism, progression to, in women drinkers, 18
Alienation and alcohol, 88
American Automobile Association, 79-80
American Drinking Practices Study, 12, 16-17
American Medical Association Committee on Alcoholism, 18
Automobile accidents, 23
  and blood alcohol concentrations, 70-71

B

BAC; *see* Blood alcohol concentration
Behavior, disruptive; *see* Disruptive behavior
Behavioral studies of alcohol education, 9-10
Biochemical action and alcohol-related aggression, 24
Biological dimension of alcohol use, 39-56
  alcohol absorption as, 41-43
  alcoholic beverages and, 40-41
  blood alcohol concentration and, 43-44
  effects of alcohol and, 45-47
  effects on specific organs or functions, 49-54
  metabolism of alcohol and, 47-49
  pharmacological properties and, 39-40
Blacks, drinking practices of, 17
Blood alcohol concentration, 11
  in laboratory assessments, 6
  measurement of, 43-45
Body size and blood alcohol concentration, 43-44
Buffalo Area Council of Alcoholism, 78

C

Cancer and alcohol, 51
Cardiomyopathy, 52-53
Cardiovascular disease, 52

INDEX

Central nervous system
  damage to, 36
  depressant effect of alcohol on, 45
Chemicals in alcoholic beverages and alcohol absorption, 41-42
Cirrhosis of liver, 49-50
Cognitive dissonance in modification of alcohol-related behavior, 57
Cognitive information, 117-125
Cognitive performance, 62-65
Cognitive phase of activated health education, 29-73
College students
  aggression, alcohol-related, in, 22
  drinking practices of, 15-16
  drinking problems and low self-concept in, 87
  and parents and drinking, relationship of, 16
Commitment to new behaviors in affective instruction, 82-83
Communication and behavior change, risk taking in, in affective instruction, 82
Consumers of health services, role of, 3-4
Coronary heart disease, 52-53
Criminal activity, alcohol-related, 21
Critical illness, 32-33
  physiological and psychosocial characteristics of, 35-36

D

Dehydrogenase and alcohol in liver, 48
Delinquent adolescents, 21-22
Delirium tremens, 36
Dependence, physical, on alcohol, 34-35
Depressant effect of alcohol, 65
  on central nervous system, 45
  and sexuality, 50-51
Depressive disorders, women drinkers with, 18
Disease process, 31-38
  health status continuum in, 31-33
Disruptive behavior, 21-27; *see also* Aggression
  aggression as, 23-25
  automobile accidents as, 23
  criminal activity as, 21
  student problems as, 21-22
Distillation process and alcohol content, 41
Divorce and alcohol-related problems, 89
Dominance in alcoholic husbands and wives, 89-90
Drinking drivers, 44-47, 60, 62, 67-69
Drinking population, 11-20
Drinking practices
  of adolescents, 13-15; *see also* Adolescents
  of blacks, 17
  classification of, 11-12
  of college students, 15-16
  of ethnic groups, 16-17

Drinking practices—cont'd
  of general population, 12
  of women, 17-18; *see also* Sex differences
Drinking practices continuum (activity), 102
Drivers, drinking, 44-47, 60, 62, 67-69
  performance skill of, 72
Driving skills and alcohol; *see* Drivers, drinking
Drugs, illicit, and alcohol, 13-14

E

Educational level of parents and drinking practices among college students, 16
Embryotoxin, alcohol as, 18
Emotional state and alcohol absorption, 43
Epinephrine secretion and alcohol-related aggression, 24
Ethanol; *see* Ethyl alcohol
Ethnic groups, drinking practices of, 16-17
Ethyl alcohol
  as central nervous system depressant, 40
  chemical structure of, 39
Evaluation, 8-9
Evaluation activity, affective, 103-107
Expectation as factor in alcohol-related aggression, 25
Experiential phase, 1-27
Experimental evidence of alcohol effects, 57-73
Expression and feeling, openness to, in affective instruction, 81

F

Fatty liver disease, 50
Feelings
  and expression, openness to, in affective instruction, 81
  nonjudgmental acceptance of, in affective instruction, 81
"Feelings" word description exercise (activity), 96-97
Fermentation process, 40
Fetal abnormalities and maternal alcohol use, 53-54
Fetal alcohol syndrome, 54
First impressions exercise (activity), 94-95

G

Gallup survey of drinking practices, 12
Games People Play, 97-100
Gastritis caused by alcohol, 50
Group activities in activated health education, 93-107
Growth deficiencies and maternal alcohol use, 53-54

H

Harris and Associates survey of drinking practices, 12
Health, optimal, 31-32
Health care, providers of, role of, 3
Health education, activated; see Activated health education
Health educator, role of, 3-4
Health services, consumers of, role of, 3-4
Health status continuum, 31-33
  and alcohol abuse, 34-47
Hearing impairment, alcohol-related, 60-62
Heart disease, 52-53
Heavy drinkers, 11-12
Hepatitis, alcohol, 50
Home accidents, 70, 72
How do you feel bingo (activity), 78
Humor preference, 59
Husbands, alcoholic, dependency on wives, 89-90

I

Ideal vs. real drinking behavior (activity), 103
Illness
  critical, 32-33
  incipient, 32
  overt, 32-33
Impaired individual, 11
Inadequacy in problem drinkers, 87
Incipient illness, 32
  physiological and psychosocial characteristics of, 35
Income, family, and drinking
  among adolescents, 13-14
  among college students, 15-16
Infrequent drinkers, 11-12
Intervention strategy, 8
Intoxicated individual, 11

K

Krebs cycle in alcohol oxidation, 49

L

Laennec's cirrhosis, 49-50
Life experiences and affective instruction, 82
Light drinkers, 11-12
Lipids, accumulation of, in liver, 50
Liver
  fatty, disease, 50
  oxidation of alcohol by, 47-48
Los Angeles Study, 52

M

Marital problems and drinking, 89-90
Metabolism of alcohol, 47-49

Microcephaly and maternal alcohol use, 54
Moderate drinkers, 11-12
Mood level and blood alcohol concentration, 45-46, 58-59
More than hello exercise (activity), 93-94
Morehead State University, alcohol awareness program at, 80
Muscle tension, 59-60

N

National Institute on Alcohol Abuse and Alcoholism, 21
Nationality and drinking practices, 16-17
Neurological disorders, alcohol-related, 36
New York State Alcohol Curriculum Guides, 78
NYSACG; see New York State Alcohol Curriculum Guides

O

Openness to expression and feeling in affective instruction, 81
Optimal health, 31-32
  physiological and psychosocial characteristics of, 34
Overt illness, 32-33
  physiological and psychosocial characteristics of, 34
Oxidation of alcohol, 48-49

P

Pedestrian accidents, blood alcohol concentrations in victims of, 69-70
Peer group pressure, 88-89
Penile tumescence and diameter, and alcohol, 50-51
Pharmacological properties of alcohol, 39-40
Physiological effects of alcohol, 6
  and blood alcohol concentrations, 34-36, 45-46
  during pregnancy, 18
Population
  drinking, 11-20
  general, drinking practices of, 12
Power and drinking behavior, 24
Powerlessness, alienation, and alcohol, 88
Pregnancy, 18, 53-54
Problem drinking, 11
Providers of health care, role of, 3
Psychological needs and alcohol use, 90-91
Psychomotor performance, 62-65
Psychosocial components of activated health education, 85-92
Pylorospasm and alcohol absorption, 43

Q

Question ranking (activity), 79

R

Racial differences in alcohol-related cancer mortality, 51
Rapid eye movement sleep and alcohol, 51-52
Rate of consumption, effect of, on alcohol absorption, 41
Reaction and choice reaction time, 65-66
Rehabilitation facilities for women drinkers, 18
Reinforced activity, drinking as, 90
Research related to activated health education, 9-10
Residence of college students and drinking practices, 15
Risk taking
  in communication and behavior change in affective instruction, 82
  in drivers, 68-69

S

Second Report to Congress on Alcohol and Health, 51
Self-concept
  negative, in women and abstainers, 18
  in problem drinkers, 86-87
Sentence completions (activity), 79
Sex differences
  and alienation, 88
  and blood alcohol concentration, 45
  and drinking, 18
    among adolescents, 14
Sex hormone level changes and alcohol, 53
Sex roles and alcohol-related aggression, 24
Sexual imagery during drinking, 24
Sexual problems, women drinkers and, 18
Sexuality and alcohol, 49-51
Sheppard Foundation Study, 22
Significance, levels of, in experimental evidence, 57-58
Sleep patterns, alcohol-related, 52
Social drinking situations exercise (activity), 101
Social Research Group, 11
Stomach
  condition of, and alcohol absorption, 42-43
  effect of alcohol on, 50

T

Tecumseh Health Study, 52
Teenagers; *see* Adolescents
Testosterone level changes and alcohol, 53
Theory and principles of activated health education, 3-8
Tolerance, physical, to alcohol, 34-35
Traffic situations, perception of, and alcohol, 68; *see also* Automobile accidents; Drivers, drinking

W

Wernicke syndrome, 36
Wives, dependence of alcoholic husbands on, 89-90
Women
  drinking practices of, 17-18
  with drinking problems, low self-concept in, 87

V

Vision impairment, alcohol-related, 60-62